THE NERVOUS SYSTEM SOLUTION

SOMATIC THERAPY APPROACH TO NAVIGATE
TRAUMA, BREAK FREE FROM ADDICTION, AND
RESTORE YOUR BODY TO FIND LASTING FREEDOM

M. SALLIE

Copyright © 2025 by M. Sallie

All rights reserved. No part of this publication may be reproduced, distributed, stored in a retrieval system, or transmitted in any form or by any means—electronic, mechanical, photocopying, recording, scanning, or otherwise—without the prior written permission of the author or publisher, except in the case of brief quotations embodied in critical reviews, academic works, or articles, provided full attribution is given.

First Edition: 2025

Cover design by *didiwahyudi.trend*

This publication is intended for informational, educational, and entertainment purposes only. It does not constitute professional medical, psychological, therapeutic, or legal advice. The author and publisher make no representations or warranties concerning the accuracy or applicability of the content contained in this book.

Do not interpret any reference to specific health practices, including but not limited to vitamins, supplements, dietary routines, or somatic therapies, as medical advice or a substitute for consultation with licensed healthcare providers. Always seek guidance from a qualified medical or mental health professional before changing your health, wellness, or treatment regimen.

Neither the author nor the publisher shall be held liable for any loss, damage, or injury allegedly arising from any information or suggestion in this book.

All characters, stories, and personal experiences described herein are either the product of the author's imagination, used with permission, or adapted to protect confidentiality. Any resemblance to actual persons, living or dead, is purely coincidental unless otherwise stated

CONTENTS

Introduction	7
1. ROOTED IN THE BODY – A GROUNDED INTRODUCTION TO SOMATIC THERAPY	9
The Roots of Somatic Therapy: Healing Addiction Through the Body	10
Understanding the Mind-Body Connection: Why Trauma Lives in the Body	12
Somatic Therapy in Recovery: Who It's For and Why It Matters	15
2. KEY PRINCIPLES OF SOMATIC THERAPY (THROUGH THE LENS OF TRAUMA AND ADDICTION)	18
Healing Begins with Reconnection	18
Listening to the Body: Learning the Language of Sensation	24
Taking It Slow: Feeling Without Flooding	25
3. PATHWAYS TO HEALING: SOMATIC APPROACHES THAT SUPPORT ADDICTION RECOVERY	27
Somatic Approaches to Addiction Recovery	28
Reiki as a Somatic Bridge in Addiction Recovery	31
Rebuilding Safety: Regulation as the Core of Recovery	33
Building Embodied Resilience: Staying Present Without Numbing	34
4. BEFORE THE STEPS - PREPARING THE BODY FOR RECOVERY WORK	36
Why the Body Comes First	36
What Trauma Does to the Nervous System	37
Is My Body Ready for the Steps?	38
Somatic Tools for Grounding and Regulation	39
Setting Up a Somatic Practice for the Steps Ahead	41

5. STEP ONE: IN THE BODY – ADMITTING
POWERLESSNESS AS A SOMATIC SURRENDER   44
The Felt Sense of Powerlessness   44
Step One in the Flesh: When Shame Lives in the Body   45
Somatic Acceptance: The First Step Toward Real
Change   46

6. STEP TWO: RECLAIMING HOPE THROUGH THE
BODY, TRUSTING IN CONNECTION, SAFETY, AND
SOMETHING MORE   51
Hope Requires Physiological Safety   52
Belief Begins in the Body   53
A Glimpse of Sanity   55

7. STEP THREE: LETTING GO OF CONTROL AS A
PHYSICAL PRACTICE   58
Surrender Is a Felt Experience   58
When Letting Go Feels Like Losing Control   59
My Story: Turning It Over, My Way   61

8. STEPS FOUR: REVISITING THE PAST SOMATICALLY   65
Emotional Inventory Can Trigger Trauma Responses   65
Listening to the Body's Version of the Story   66
Somatic Practice: Inventory Walk – Releasing Shadows
with the Earth   69
Staying Present When the Past Arises   71

9. STEP FIVE: FEELING THE PAST TO FINALLY
RELEASE IT   73
Step Five Becomes a Nervous System Release   73
Confession as a Full-Body Surrender   74
Where the Body Speaks: Walking Out What Was Buried   75

10. STEP SIX: RELEASING DEFENSES, NOT JUST
DEFECTS   79
Character Defects as Protective Adaptations   79
The Nervous System Defends Against Past Harm   80
Somatic Practice: Water Release Ritual – Surrendering
Old Survival Strategies   81
Becoming Ready, One Breath at a Time   83

11. STEP SEVEN: THE SOMATIC WEIGHT OF
"CHARACTER DEFECTS"   86
The Somatic Weight of Shortcomings   86
The Somatic Surrender   87

12. STEP EIGHT: THE BODY REMEMBERS, AND SO DO
    OTHERS ... 92
    Others Remember, Too ... 92
    Pain Doesn't Live in a Vacuum, and Neither Does
    Healing ... 93
    Preparing the Body for Relational Repair: A Somatic
    Approach to Step Eight ... 94
    Humility as Relational Surrender ... 97
    Slow Repair and Somatic Grace ... 98

13. STEP NINE: REPAIR WITH PRESENCE ... 100
    The Body Must Be Ready to Return ... 100
    Repair Happens in the Nervous System First ... 101
    Somatic Practice for Step Nine: The Embodied Amends ... 103
    Owning the Impact Without Needing Redemption ... 104
    Living Amends, Sacred Repair ... 105

14. LIVING THE STEPS THROUGH THE BODY: STEPS
    TEN, ELEVEN, AND TWELVE ... 109
    Step Ten: Embodied Self-Reflection ... 109
    Step Ten as a Practice of Presence ... 111

15. BEYOND THE STEPS – A SOMATIC PATH FOR
    EVERY RECOVERY JOURNEY ... 120
    Why the Body Belongs in Every Recovery Story ... 121
    What Somatic Recovery Can Look Like (No Steps
    Required) ... 123
    Staying Regulated – Preventing Relapse Through
    Somatic Integration ... 130

16. EMBODIED SPIRITUALITY - GOD, THE BODY, AND
    THE SOUL ... 133
    When God Isn't What You Thought ... 133
    The Body as the Temple ... 134
    Becoming a Vessel ... 135

17. HEALING IN REAL TIME - PERSONAL JOURNEYS OF
    SOBRIETY AND SAFETY ... 138
    A Therapist's Story: Bearing Witness Through the Body ... 142

18. WHEN THE BODY REACHES BACK – A SOMATIC
    VIEW OF RELAPSE ... 145
    Before the Slip: The Somatic Storm No One Sees ... 146
    The Disconnection Phase: When the Body Stops
    Speaking Softly ... 146

The Internal Pressure Cooker: When the Body Can't Hold It All	148
Early Craving as a Call for Contact	149
The Repair Phase: Reconnecting After the Storm	153
After the Fall: Shame, Shutdown, and the Silence That Follows	154
19. BOUNDARIES, TRIGGERS, AND SAFETY	158
The Nervous System Craves Safety, Not Control	159
Understanding Triggers: What They Really Are	160
Boundary Work Is Recovery Work	166
20. TRUSTING THE BODY AGAIN	175
The Body Was Never the Enemy – It Was the Messenger	175
21. PRACTICAL TECHNIQUES FOR HEALING AND RECOVERY	184
The Power of Ritual: Making Healing Tangible	184
New Practice: The 5-4-3-2-1 Nature Reset	186
Why Routine Matters for the Nervous System	187
22. LONG-TERM RECOVERY AND THE EMBODIED SELF	192
The Moment It Changed	193
Writing to the Body That Stayed	193
Touch, Movement, and Stillness: Returning Through the Senses	194
23. A NEW KIND OF SOBRIETY	197
Beyond Abstinence—The Embodied Awakening	197
A Legacy Written in the Body	199
Glossary of Somatic and Recovery Terms	205
References	211

INTRODUCTION

I enjoyed many moments while drinking. That's the part people don't always talk about at first. I laughed harder, danced more, and connected faster. It worked until it didn't. Eventually, I was waking up in places I didn't recognize, with shame that clung to my skin and anxiety that no shower could wash off. The drink that once gave me life started taking it from me.

I've been through more detoxes than I can count, in and out of rehabs. I've made promises I meant and broken them days later. Each time I got out, I swore it would be different. I'd attend meetings, find a sponsor, read the Big Book, and fully commit to the Steps. And I want to be clear: those things have saved my life. The AA program, fellowship, and structure are sacred ground. I wouldn't be here without it. If you're reading this and AA is part of your path, I see you. Keep going.

But even with all that, I couldn't shake a gnawing sense of discontent. I'd put the drink down, but I still woke up with dread. I still felt unsafe in my own skin. I was sober, but I wasn't at peace. Something in me was still twisted tight, braced for impact, always on edge.

That's when I started to learn about the *allergy of the body and the obsession of the mind* and how trauma plays into both. AA calls it a spiritual malady, and I agree. But I've come to believe that part of that spiritual disconnection begins in the body. Because if the body doesn't feel safe, it can't trust. It can't soften. And if it can't soften, it can't surrender.

Somatic theory changed everything for me. I began to understand that my nervous system wasn't just dysregulated; it was trapped in survival mode. I wasn't defective or weak. I was wired for danger, for shutdown, for fight or flight. And no amount of white-knuckling could heal that. I needed to listen to my body, not override it.

This book isn't here to replace AA or to discredit it; it's here to *support it*. To deepen it. To give you tools to address the parts of you that are still holding on for dear life even after the drinking stops.

True sobriety isn't just about not picking up. It's about feeling safe in your body again. It's about reconnecting with yourself, your spirit, your truth, your breath. That's where real healing begins.

In the pages that follow, we'll explore how somatic practices can help you rewire your nervous system, release stored trauma, and create the internal safety that makes spiritual awakening possible. We'll look at how the body holds on to pain, how it can let go, and how that release opens the door to freedom, not just from substances but from the suffering that made them necessary in the first place.

If you're still searching for that missing piece like I was, I hope this book becomes a part of your journey home. Because sobriety is not just about staying sober; it's about becoming whole.

1

ROOTED IN THE BODY – A GROUNDED INTRODUCTION TO SOMATIC THERAPY

Addiction is often described as a disease of the mind or spirit. Still, many people overlook one of the most essential parts of the healing equation: the body. For those in recovery, the body is often where the pain lives the loudest, even long after substances are gone. Restlessness, numbness, anxiety, physical tension, and emotional overwhelm are not just side effects of quitting; They are signs that the nervous system is dysregulated, *meaning it's stuck in survival mode, unable to return to a state of calm or balance*, and still carrying the imprint of unresolved trauma."

Somatic therapy offers a new way forward. It doesn't focus on "fixing" you or analyzing your past. Instead, it helps you feel safe in your body again, which, for many people in recovery, is something they've never experienced. If addiction numbs, distracts, or dissociates, somatic therapy helps you reconnect, regulate, and reclaim your internal world, one sensation at a time.

THE ROOTS OF SOMATIC THERAPY: HEALING ADDICTION THROUGH THE BODY

The idea that healing must involve the body is not new, but only in recent decades has it begun to receive the attention it deserves, especially in the world of addiction recovery. For years, therapy focused mainly on thoughts, behaviors, and emotions. But for those of us who have struggled with addiction, that approach often left something untouched, something still restless, still aching, still unresolved. That something is the body.

Somatic therapy began taking shape nearly a century ago when Austrian psychiatrist Wilhelm Reich, once a student of Freud, suggested that emotional trauma didn't just exist in the mind. He observed that people held their pain physically in tense muscles, rigid posture, and shallow breathing. He called it "muscular armoring," a protective response to years of repression, hurt, or fear. Reich believed that if therapy ignored the body, it ignored a crucial part of how trauma lives inside us. At the time, his ideas were radical. But his core belief, that the body holds memory would go on to influence some of the most critical trauma and addiction work in modern history.

Decades later, Alexander Lowen, a physician and psychotherapist, expanded on Reich's work by developing a method called Bioenergetic Analysis. His approach helped people release the physical blocks caused by suppressed emotion, which he believed was the frozen energy of unexpressed pain. For those living with addiction, his work offered a new understanding: that the compulsion to use substances was often linked to deeply buried emotional wounds that had never found expression. These wounds weren't just psychological; they had shape, weight, and presence inside the body. They were stored in clenched jaws, collapsed shoulders, and the numbness in the chest that told a person it wasn't safe to feel.

Still, the clinical world had not yet entirely accepted the idea that trauma was a body-based experience. That shift began with the work of Dr. Peter Levine. In the 1970s, Levine studied how animals respond to life-threatening events. After escaping danger, animals would often shake, tremble, or release tension before returning to a calm state. Humans, he noticed, didn't do this. We shut down. We override. We go numb. His groundbreaking insight was this: trauma doesn't come from the event itself but from the nervous system's inability to complete its natural survival response. When we freeze and never thaw, that energy stays trapped, driving fear, anxiety, and, yes, addictive behaviors. To heal, we must learn to listen to what our bodies are still holding on to. Peter Levine's method, Somatic Experiencing, helps people gently reconnect with the physical responses their body couldn't complete during trauma, like the urge to run, fight, or cry. The goal isn't to relive the past but to finally allow the body to finish what it once had to freeze or suppress, bringing a sense of resolution and relief, often for the first time.

This shift toward body-based healing gained even more ground with the research of Dr. Bessel van der Kolk. Through brain scans, clinical practice, and decades of work with trauma survivors, van der Kolk proved what so many people in recovery already know deep down: trauma changes the brain, alters the body, and creates patterns of behavior that can't simply be reasoned away. His now-famous book, *The Body Keeps the Score*, makes the case that trauma resides in the nervous system, in the muscles, and in the very cells of our being. And that unless we involve the body in healing, recovery remains incomplete. Van der Kolk didn't just validate somatic therapy; he helped shift the entire field of trauma and addiction treatment toward embodied care.

Today, somatic therapy is being embraced in treatment centers, trauma-informed programs, and recovery communities around the world. And the reason is simple: it works. For many people in addiction recovery, the pain didn't start with the first drink or drug. It began earlier, with the fear that haunted the home, the loneliness that never left, and the shame that had settled into the bones. Addiction was not the beginning; it was a way to survive what the body could no longer carry. Somatic therapy helps us return to those frozen places with care. It teaches us that our bodies weren't betraying us; they were protecting us. And now, with the proper support, they can begin to release.

Studies show that the vast majority of people in addiction recovery, some estimates suggest over seventy percent, have experienced significant trauma. And yet, many traditional recovery models still focus only on behavior and abstinence. Somatic therapy brings us back to the root. It offers a way to feel again without being overwhelmed. It teaches us how to stay present when the urge to run is strong. It helps us build safety from the inside out, so sobriety isn't something we fight for; it's something we can finally feel at home in.

The history of somatic therapy is, in many ways, the history of returning to ourselves. And for those of us who have used substances to escape the pain that lives in our bodies, it offers a new path. Not a quick fix or a miracle cure, but a steady, compassionate process of listening, noticing, and healing. Through this lens, recovery becomes more than just staying sober; it is a transformative journey of self-discovery. By restoring awareness to the body and allowing for slow, safe reconnection to sensation, Somatic Theory gives recovering individuals a new path that doesn't shame their pain. Still, it helps them move through it, one breath at a time.

UNDERSTANDING THE MIND-BODY CONNECTION: WHY TRAUMA LIVES IN THE BODY

A Story of Hidden Wounds

Carlos grew up with a tense stomach and a racing mind, but no apparent reason why. He was a quiet kid in a chaotic home: yelling matches, slammed doors, and the ever-present knot in his gut. As an adult, stress made his neck and shoulders seize up, and he found himself craving a drink each evening just to relax. Weekends of heavy drinking slowly turned into a constant dependency. Even after entering recovery and giving up alcohol, Carlos still woke up in the night drenched in sweat and anxiety. He finally realized that something deeper was hurting him, not just in his thoughts but in his body. Through therapy, Carlos learned that his body had never really let go of the fear and tension from his childhood. In one session of somatic therapy, a gentle guided exercise helped him place a hand on his chest and breathe slowly; he felt a little of his tightness begin to ease. For the first time, he understood that the unresolved pain, the trauma, had been *stuck* in his body all along. This gave him hope that he could slowly unwind those old knots without feeling overwhelmed.

Trauma's Impact on the Body and Brain

The way Carlos's body reacted is not unusual. When we face real danger, our brain sounds an alarm that zaps our body with stress hormones. A sudden threat, even an emotional one, causes the heart to pound, breathing to quicken, and muscles to tense ("fight-or-flight" mode). This response helped our ancestors survive predators and wars. But when stress is chronic (like ongoing abuse or neglect), the body stays on high alert long after the danger is gone. Over time, that constant "foot on the gas pedal" wears us out physically. Chronic stress can even change brain function and is linked to anxiety, depression, and addiction. In other words, the very systems that kept Carlos safe as a child were still revving even when he was safe as an adult, fueling his anxiety and cravings.

Somatic therapists refer to these held sensations *as somatic memories*. If a body cannot fully complete its natural fight, flight or freeze reaction, the leftover energy can become trapped in tissues and cells. As Amanda Baker of Harvard explains, trauma is not just in our minds – our bodies hold it, too. "Somatic therapies posit that our body holds and expresses experiences and emotions, and traumatic events or unresolved emotional issues can become 'trapped' inside." That tension might show up as knots in muscles, stomach aches, headaches, or a jittery heart that won't quiet. It's as if the body is still protecting us from the past threat, even when no danger is present.

Fortunately, this body-mind link also points to a path forward. Somatic therapy works with the body's natural processes to release that held tension. Instead of just talking through emotions, it guides us to gently notice where we feel stress in our body and safely discharge it. For example, a therapist might have you close your eyes, place a hand on your heart, and take slow, deep breaths. Simple practices like this help calm the nervous system and remind the body that it *is* now safe. Over time, as the body learns it can relax, the chronic "gas pedal" response eases up, and the feelings of anxiety or pain can soften.

Somatic therapy often starts with calm, body-based practices. In sessions, people might sit quietly with their eyes closed, place a hand on their chest, and take gentle breathsthemeadows.com. By tuning into simple sensations (like the rise and fall of the breath) and using techniques such as grounding or guided imagery, the body's stress response can gradually unwind. These mind-body practices teach the nervous system to move from a state of tension toward a state of relaxation.

Building on these simple exercises, somatic therapy gradually teaches skills that empower healing. For someone like Carlos, learning to pay attention to his body signals eventually broke the cycle of anxiety and substance use. With practice, he could feel an old panic in his stomach and respond by slowing down his breath, rather than reaching for alcohol. He also learned to recognize safe, calming images or memories that brought a genuine sense of ease (a technique called **resourcing**). Bit by bit, the trapped trauma began to lose its grip on him.

Somatic therapy can help you learn to:

- **Tune into your body's signals.** Notice where tension or discomfort lives (aches in your shoulders, a pit in your stomach, a racing heart) and use simple tools like deep breathing or gentle movement to soothe it.
- **Release stress safely.** Through guided exercises (such as stretching, rocking, or allowing subtle body tremors), you gradually discharge the stuck energy of trauma without becoming overwhelmed.

- **Build a sense of safety.** Techniques such as *pendulation* (shifting attention between calm and stressful sensations) and *resourcing* (recalling a supportive memory or place) help train the nervous system to feel safe in the body againhealth.harvard.edu.
- **Manage intense emotions and cravings.** By calming your nervous system, you gain tools to handle anger, fear, or urges more skillfully. Over time, you become more aware of early warning signs of anxiety or cravings and can choose healthier responsesthemeadows.comthemeadows.com.
- **Rebuild mind-body connection.** You learn to trust your body again. As chronic tension and pain ease, sleep and energy improve, and you can live more fully in the present moment.

Together, these skills help break the cycle that held Carlos (and many others) captive. Trauma no longer rules the body alone; the person learns to gently reclaim control over their own body. This understanding that trauma is as much physical as mental lays the foundation for real healing. In the next chapter, we'll explore specific somatic exercises and practices that continue this journey, helping you release what's been stored and move forward with hope and strength.

SOMATIC THERAPY IN RECOVERY: WHO IT'S FOR AND WHY IT MATTERS

Somatic therapy is for anyone who wants to feel more at home in their body. Still, it is especially powerful for those recovering from addiction. Many people in sobriety find that once the substance is removed, the real work begins. Anxiety, panic, shame, flashbacks, or dissociation can flood in, and without tools to manage those states, relapse becomes more likely.

Somatic therapy helps people in recovery by teaching them how to:

- **Notice triggers in the body before they escalate.** Somatic awareness enables you to catch dysregulation early before it spirals into cravings or self-sabotage.
- **Cope with emotional intensity without numbing.** Instead of reaching for a drink or drug, somatic tools help you breathe, move, or ground yourself through the storm.
- **Repair trust with the body.** Addiction often teaches you to ignore or override your body's signals. Somatic work rebuilds that trust, one small step at a time.
- **Transform shame into self-compassion.** Many people in recovery carry deep shame, not just for what they did while using, but for how they feel in their bodies. Somatic therapy helps you meet that shame with care, not judgment.
- **Anchor sobriety in the body, not just the willpower.** Lasting recovery is about feeling safe enough to stay sober. Somatic tools help you build that safety from within, so sobriety isn't just something you force—it's something your whole being can support.

Whether you're newly sober or years into recovery, if you still feel unsettled in your body, if you're stuck in patterns of tension, emotional flooding, or shutdown, somatic therapy may be the missing piece.

Chapter Summary

Addiction often begins as an attempt to escape pain the body has never been allowed to fully feel. For many, sobriety brings clarity but also reveals the deep discomfort, dysregulation, and unresolved trauma that substances once masked. In Chapter One, we explored how somatic therapy reframes addiction not as a moral failure but as a body-based survival response, a way the nervous system copes when no other tools are available.

We examined the origins of somatic therapy, from the pioneering work of Wilhelm Reich and Alexander Lowen to the trauma-informed breakthroughs of Peter Levine and Bessel van der Kolk. These clinicians and researchers helped reshape the way we understand addiction and healing, moving beyond talk therapy to recognize the vital role of the body in trauma recovery. Their insights form the foundation of an approach that sees healing not as a mental effort alone but as a full-bodied return to safety, presence, and wholeness.

This chapter introduced the key principle that healing requires us to come back into our bodies, learn their language, listen to their signals, and support them with compassion. When the body becomes an ally, not an enemy, sobriety transforms from something we fight for to something we begin to trust and live from.

But to truly walk this path, we need more than just insight; we need a foundation. In the next chapter, we'll explore the core principles of somatic therapy through the lens of trauma and addiction. You'll learn how the body responds to overwhelm, why it holds on to pain long after the moment has passed, and how somatic healing creates real, lasting change. This is where the deeper work begins.

2

KEY PRINCIPLES OF SOMATIC THERAPY (THROUGH THE LENS OF TRAUMA AND ADDICTION)

HEALING BEGINS WITH RECONNECTION

When we talk about somatic therapy in the context of addiction and trauma, we're talking about healing the body that learned to survive by disconnecting. For many of us, that disconnection didn't happen all at once; it happened slowly, quietly, and for good reason. Our bodies shut down certain sensations, emotions, and instincts, not because we were weak, but because it was the only way to endure what was too overwhelming to face.

Take Marcus, for example. From the outside, his drinking looked like self-destruction. But underneath, it was how he managed the emotional aftermath of childhood neglect. As a boy, he had learned that crying didn't bring comfort, that speaking up made things worse, and that the safest place to be was invisible. By the time he was a teenager, he'd mastered the art of checking out, first with food, then with alcohol. His body had learned to go numb before he even realized he was upset.

Years later, in recovery, Marcus wasn't drinking, but he still couldn't feel much. When someone asked how he was, he'd shrug. He didn't know. His emotions were static. His body stayed tense, his breath shallow. It wasn't until he began somatic therapy that he realized how deeply his body had armored itself against life. Somatic work didn't ask him to explain everything. It asked him to notice his clenched fists, his stiff spine, and the way his chest didn't rise when he inhaled. And little by little, as he began to feel what had been locked away for so long, he also began to feel more alive.

This is what somatic therapy offers. A way back into the body, not to overwhelm, but to repair. Not to relive trauma but to gently complete the survival responses that were cut short. Through this process, healing becomes more than just a concept. It becomes something you can actually feel: in your breath, in your posture, in your ability to stay present when things get hard.

Now that we understand the need let's look at the core principles that guide this work.

1. Addiction Is a Body-Based Survival Strategy

Most people don't turn to substances because life feels good. They turn to them because life feels *unbearable*. Because their body is flooded with pain, fear, shame, or emptiness, and they need a way out. Addiction, from a somatic lens, isn't just about bad choices or weak willpower. It's about a nervous system overwhelmed by trauma, stress, or chronic emotional pain that never had a safe place to land.

Alcohol, drugs, sex, food, gambling, chaos, they all offer something that feels like relief. They slow things down. They numb what hurts. They offer control when everything inside feels out of control. In a body stuck in fight, flight, freeze, or collapse, substances become a fast way to soothe what feels unmanageable. Not because they're healthy, but because, for a time, *they work*.

Somatic therapy doesn't shame you for that. It honors the brilliance of your survival. It says: *Of course, you reached for something to help you cope. Of course, your body did what it needed to do to survive.* That reframe is powerful. It allows us to view addiction not as a failure but as an adaptation.

Take Luis, for example. He started using painkillers after a sports injury in college. But what hooked him wasn't the high; it was the silence. For the first time in his life, the constant anxiety in his chest disappeared. He didn't have to think about the abuse he'd survived as a kid, or the pressure to perform, or the fear of not being good enough. His addiction wasn't about getting wasted; it was about finally feeling *nothing*. His nervous system had never known a moment of peace. Drugs gave him a version of it until they took everything else away.

That's why recovery has to go deeper than just stopping the behavior. Sobriety alone doesn't teach the body how to feel safe. It just removes the thing that was helping you cope. That's where somatic therapy steps in to help you slowly build a sense of safety that doesn't depend on escaping yourself.

True healing starts not with judgment but with understanding. When you begin to see your addiction as a response to suffering, not as a flaw, you also begin to see recovery not as punishment but as the process of returning home to your body with compassion and care.

2. Trauma Lives in the Nervous System, Not Just in Memory

When people hear the word *trauma*, they often think of the event itself: what happened, when, where, and how. But in somatic therapy, trauma isn't defined by the event alone. It's defined by what *happened inside you* in response to that event and what your body had to do to survive it.

Even when your mind says, *'That was a long time ago,'* your body might still be acting as if it's happening right now. That's because trauma gets stored in the nervous system. It appears not just as memories but as muscle tension that won't go away. As numbness in your chest. As a constant need to stay busy or a deep fear of being touched, even by someone safe. You might not even *remember* everything that happened, but your body does.

This was true for Tasha. She had been sober for six months and doing everything "right": going to meetings, working the Steps, and staying close to her sponsor. But she couldn't shake the feeling that something was still wrong. She couldn't sleep. Her chest was always tight. And whenever someone touched her arm unexpectedly, even gently, her whole body would freeze. She didn't understand it until one day she finally shared in the group that she had been sexually assaulted at the age of seventeen. She had told herself it "wasn't that bad" that she had moved on. But her body hadn't. It was still bracing. Still waiting for the next violation.

That's what trauma does. It doesn't always live in your thoughts; it lives in your tissues. It lives in your breath, your reactions, and your startle reflex. For people in recovery, this can make sobriety incredibly confusing. You've taken away the substance, but your body still feels unsafe. Still overwhelmed. Still on edge. And so the craving returns—not just for alcohol or drugs, but for *relief*.

Somatic therapy helps us find that relief, not by talking about what happened over and over, but by slowly helping the body *complete* what it couldn't do back then. To tremble, to cry, to push away, to breathe again. It's not about reliving the pain; it's about giving your body the chance to *resolve* it.

When trauma is processed at the level of the nervous system, something shifts. Triggers lose their grip. Your body begins to feel less like a war zone and more like a place you can actually live in. And that, more than any explanation or insight, is what opens the door to real, lasting peace.

3. Regulation Is the Foundation of Recovery

One of the biggest challenges in sobriety is learning how to feel without being consumed by what we feel. Early recovery often brings a flood of emotions we used to numb or avoid—fear, anger, sadness, shame. Without alcohol or other substances to dull the edges, even small triggers can feel overwhelming. This is where somatic therapy introduces one of its most essential concepts: **regulation**.

Regulation is the ability to notice when your nervous system is shifting into a survival state, such as fight, flight, or freeze, and to gently bring yourself back to a state of steadiness. It's not about suppressing emotions or pretending everything's fine. It's about recognizing what's happening in your body and having the tools to calm the storm before it takes over.

For example, suppose your heart starts racing after a tense conversation. In that case, regulation might look like placing your hand over your chest and taking slow, deep breaths. If you feel yourself shutting down emotionally, it may mean grounding through your feet, noticing the support of the floor beneath you, or gently moving your body to release frozen energy. These simple practices help your body shift out of automatic protection and back into presence.

Regulation is not about perfection; it's about building a new relationship with your nervous system. One where you don't have to be ruled by reactivity. One where you can feel without falling apart. And over time, as regulation becomes more familiar, it creates the stability that long-term recovery depends on.

Regulation isn't just about calming down. It's about being able to ride the waves of emotion, sensation, and memory without needing to escape. In addiction recovery, this is crucial. If you can't regulate, it's incredibly difficult to resist the pull of old habits that promised relief.

Through practices like grounding, breathwork, movement, and noticing bodily sensations, somatic therapy helps you build resilience in your nervous system, so sobriety doesn't feel like white-knuckling but like true internal stability.

4. Awareness and Safety Go Hand-in-Hand

Many people in recovery feel unsafe in their own bodies. Even after the drinking or using stops, that uneasy feeling lingers, the tension in your chest, the constant need to stay busy, the fear that if you slow down, something might break open. Years of trauma, unprocessed emotion, and survival-based coping have trained your nervous system to stay on high alert. The result? Disconnection. From your body. From your emotions. From yourself.

Somatic therapy doesn't ask you to dive straight into the deep end. It doesn't force you to face everything all at once. Instead, it starts where real healing begins: with *safety*. Not as an idea but as a felt experience. And safety always comes first.

Sometimes, that looks like something as simple as noticing your breath for five seconds. Feeling the support of a chair beneath you. Placing your hand on your heart or your belly, not to change anything, but just to say, *I'm here*. These small acts begin to re-establish a sense of presence and trust within your body. They send the message: *You're not in danger anymore. You can start to come back now.*

For example, when Maya first got sober, she struggled with overwhelming panic whenever she sat still. Her therapist asked her to try body scans or breathwork, but they made her feel worse like she was trapped. It wasn't until she learned that safety had to take precedence over awareness that things started to shift. With the help of a somatic practitioner, Maya began by simply noticing her feet on the floor while doing everyday tasks. Folding laundry. Brushing her teeth. No deep breathing. No, closing her eyes. Just *noticing*, without judgment. Over time, her body started to trust the process. She didn't need to force anything. The safety grew because it was honored.

This is the heart of somatic work: an awareness that's paced by safety. For trauma survivors, especially those in recovery, this principle is essential. You've likely spent years ignoring or overriding your body's signals just to get through the day. Somatic therapy doesn't punish you for that. It gently invites you to do something new. Something slower. Something kinder.

It says, *'Let's go at the speed of trust.' Let's listen first. Let's rebuild the relationship with your body: not through pressure, but through presence.*

5. Healing Happens Through the Body, Not Around It

You can't think your way out of trauma. You can't force your way through recovery. Real, lasting change comes when you begin to feel safe inside your own skin. That's what somatic therapy offers.

Whether you're dealing with cravings, emotional outbursts, deep shame, or the constant hum of anxiety, these are not just mental struggles. They're embodied experiences, and they need to be met with embodied solutions.

Somatic therapy helps turn your body into an ally in recovery—not something to escape, but something to come home to.

LISTENING TO THE BODY: LEARNING THE LANGUAGE OF SENSATION

After years of numbing out, Marcus didn't know how to answer when people asked how he felt. In early recovery, he still lived in a kind of fog. His body was always tense, his breath shallow, and he often felt disconnected, as if he were floating outside himself. When he started somatic therapy, the first thing his therapist asked wasn't what he remembered. It was, *"What do you notice in your body right now?"*

At first, he didn't know how to answer. But over time, he learned to tune in to small signals: a clenched jaw, a tight chest, a knot in his stomach. These weren't just random discomforts. They were messages, his body's way of saying, "I'm not okay," even when his words hadn't caught up yet.

This is called **interoception**, your ability to notice what's happening inside your body. It's a skill many people in addiction lose touch with because substances help us ignore what hurts. But when Marcus started noticing his body's cues, such as a pounding heart when he was anxious or shallow breathing when he was overwhelmed, he began to catch himself before spiraling. Instead of reaching for a drink, he learned to pause. To breathe. To ask, *"What do I really need right now?"*

Little by little, Marcus began to trust his body again. He learned that those signals weren't enemies; they were guides. His body wasn't trying to sabotage him; it was trying to help him feel, respond, and heal. And as he learned to stay present with those feelings, even the uncomfortable ones, he found himself less reactive, more grounded, and more in control, not by force, but by listening.

TAKING IT SLOW: FEELING WITHOUT FLOODING

For most of his life, Marcus thought the only way to deal with pain was to shove it down or drink it away. When he started talking about the past, everything came rushing in. Memories, fear, shame, it was too much, too fast. But his somatic therapist showed him a new way: **go slow.**

In somatic therapy, two important tools are called **titration** and **pendulation**. They're fancy words for a simple idea: you don't have to dive headfirst into your pain. You can dip in, then step back. You can feel a little, then rest. Then feel a little more. Just like working out a sore muscle, you stretch gently, not all at once.

One day, Marcus started to talk about a childhood memory that always made him freeze up. As soon as he felt the tightness in his chest, his therapist gently guided him to look around the room to find something that made him feel safe: the soft light coming through the window, the chair under his legs, his breath. Then they circled back. In and out. Back and forth. This rhythm is called pendulation, which involves moving between what's hard and what's comforting so the body doesn't become overwhelmed.

With each small step, Marcus began to feel less afraid of his own story. He didn't need to relive everything all at once. He just needed to feel what he could handle and then return to safety. That's titration, a slow release, not a flood. And slowly, the memories stopped owning him.

For people in recovery, this kind of pacing is everything. It helps you face the past without being overwhelmed by it. It teaches your nervous system that it can handle discomfort and return to a calm state. Over time, Marcus began to feel more solid. He cried and shook sometimes, but it didn't undo him. He could come back. He could stay. And that staying changed everything.

Chapter Summary

Somatic healing starts with a simple but powerful truth: your body has always been telling the story, even when your words couldn't. For many of us in recovery, the body was the first place we abandoned because it hurt too much to stay. Through addiction, we learned to numb, escape, or override our physical signals. But through somatic therapy, we begin the brave work of returning.

This chapter explored the foundational principles that guide that return. We examined how reconnection to the body is often the first step, involving learning to notice, listen, and stay present without judgment. We saw how interoception, or tuning in to the body's internal signals, helps build awareness and trust. We explored how titration and pendulation offer a path through pain that doesn't retraumatize but restores a rhythm of healing that honors your limits while expanding your capacity.

Marcus's story reminded us that healing doesn't have to be big or dramatic. Sometimes, it's as small as unclenching a fist. Taking a deep breath. Naming a sensation. Choosing to stay. These are not just coping tools; they are the building blocks of long-term recovery. They show us that we don't have to fight our bodies anymore. We can begin to live *with* them, not in fear, but in partnership.

As we move into Chapter Three, we'll take this understanding further by exploring the many somatic approaches now available to support addiction recovery. From Somatic Experiencing and EMDR to trauma-informed yoga, breathwork, and other body-based practices, we'll look at practical, research-supported methods that help regulate the nervous system, release long-held tension, and rebuild connection from the inside out. Healing from addiction is not a one-size-fits-all journey, but there *is* a path that leads through the body.

3

PATHWAYS TO HEALING: SOMATIC APPROACHES THAT SUPPORT ADDICTION RECOVERY

You did something incredible by getting sober. It's a huge milestone, but for many, it can feel like just the first step on a long journey. You may have put down the drink or drug and stayed clean for months or years, and yet something still feels off. Perhaps your body is still tense for no clear reason, or you find yourself snapping at loved ones or shutting down emotionally. You've been following all the steps, meetings, therapy, self-care, and yet true peace still feels just out of reach.

This is where body-based healing comes in. It recognizes something important: healing isn't only in the mind, but it also happens in the body.

Often, addiction starts because our bodies never felt safe. Maybe you experienced trauma, chronic stress, or pain that you didn't know how to handle. In response, you may have learned to disconnect from your feelings, your body, and even yourself. Substances gave temporary relief, but even after you stopped using them, that old pain can still feel trapped in your system.

Body-based practices work gently and safely with that stored tension. They teach you how to feel again without being overwhelmed. You learn to calm your nervous system, stay present in your body, and gradually release what you've been carrying.

These practices don't force you to relive your worst moments. Instead, they offer small, steady steps to reconnect with your body in ways that feel manageable and achievable.

You might start by simply noticing your breath or by allowing gentle movements that feel good. Pay attention to where you hold tension and let it soften. Over time, these small steps help build something addiction never could: a real sense of safety inside yourself.

In the rest of this chapter, you'll explore different body-based approaches to healing. Each one is a little different, but they all share the same goal: helping you feel more grounded, more alive, and more whole. These practices aren't quick fixes, but they can be powerful. They meet you where you are, not just with your story but with your body, too.

You've come so far by getting sober. Now, these body-based practices can be the support that helps you finally feel truly whole. For many people in long-term recovery, focusing on the body has been exactly what was missing all along.

SOMATIC APPROACHES TO ADDICTION RECOVERY

Somatic Experiencing (SE)

- Developed by Dr. Peter Levine, Somatic Experiencing (SE) helps people gently release trauma stored in the nervous system by tracking physical sensations and allowing the body to complete its natural survival responses.
- *In Recovery:* SE is beneficial for calming anxiety, reducing triggers, supporting nervous system regulation, and essential for preventing relapse.

Hakomi Method

- Created by Ron Kurtz, Hakomi uses mindfulness and body awareness to uncover unconscious beliefs stored in posture, breath, and sensation.
- *In Recovery:* It helps individuals identify and transform internal messages like "I'm not safe" or "I'm unlovable" that often drive addiction.

EMDR (Eye Movement Desensitization and Reprocessing)

- Originally designed for trauma, EMDR uses bilateral stimulation (eye movements or tapping) to help the brain reprocess distressing memories. When combined with somatic awareness, it allows the body to release stored tension alongside emotional pain.
- *In Recovery:* EMDR supports healing the root trauma behind addiction while teaching people to stay grounded in their bodies.

Bioenergetic Analysis

- Developed by Dr. Alexander Lowen, this therapy combines physical exercises, breathwork, and body awareness to release emotional blocks held in the body.
- *In Recovery:* It helps people reconnect with suppressed feelings, rebuild energy, and restore emotional expression after years of numbness.

Feldenkrais Method

- Utilizes slow, gentle movements and awareness to retrain the nervous system and enhance physical and emotional well-being.
- *In Recovery:* Offers a safe way to rebuild self-awareness, reduce tension, and develop a sense of calm presence in the body.

Alexander Technique

- Focuses on improving posture and movement efficiency through conscious awareness of bodily habits.
- *In Recovery:* Supports a deeper connection to the body, especially for those healing from chronic tension, dissociation, or shame held in physical form.

Tension & Trauma Releasing Exercises (TRE)

- Created by Dr. David Berceli, TRE uses specific physical exercises to induce natural tremors that release deep tension and trauma from the body.
- *In Recovery:* These neurogenic tremors help release stress and trauma safely, especially for those who struggle to express emotion verbally.

Trauma-Sensitive Yoga

- A form of yoga adapted for trauma survivors that focuses on gentle movement, choice, and body awareness rather than performance or flexibility.
- *In Recovery:* Provides a safe way to reconnect with the body, manage anxiety, and rebuild physical and emotional trust without judgment.

Craniosacral Therapy

- A gentle, hands-on technique that supports the body's natural rhythms and releases tension in the nervous system.
- *In Recovery:* Helps people who experience emotional shutdown, chronic fatigue, or deep stress states by promoting calm and subtle reconnection.

Rosen Method Bodywork

- It uses gentle touch and verbal interaction to release unconscious muscle tension and emotional holding patterns.
- *In Recovery:* Assists with emotional openness and reconnecting to parts of the body that feel "frozen" or numb after trauma.

Breathwork and Somatic Meditation

- Guided breathing and internal body scanning techniques that help regulate emotion and increase interoception (inner body awareness).
- *In Recovery:* Offers immediate tools for grounding, managing cravings, and re-establishing a relationship with one's internal state.

Each of these somatic approaches offers a doorway back to the body, a place many in recovery have long feared, ignored, or fled. There is no single path, and no method is right for everyone. But all share the same goal: to help you feel safe enough to stay present, to listen deeply, and to heal at the pace your nervous system can handle. In learning to work with the body rather than against it, you begin to build a foundation for lasting recovery, grounded not in willpower but in compassion, connection, and embodied resilience.

REIKI AS A SOMATIC BRIDGE IN ADDICTION RECOVERY

In the intricate journey of healing from addiction, the body often carries the imprint of unresolved trauma, showing up as chronic tension, emotional dysregulation, and persistent cravings. Somatic therapies aim to address these embodied experiences by cultivating awareness, regulating emotions, and facilitating release. Within this framework, **Reiki can serve as a gentle, supportive tool**, particularly when integrated into a broader therapeutic approach.

Reiki, a Japanese practice often translated as "universal life energy," involves light touch or hovering of the hands over the body to support relaxation and energetic balance. Though its mechanism is not yet fully understood, many clients report a sense of calm, groundedness, and relief following a session. For individuals in recovery, Reiki may offer somatic benefits such as:

- **Promoting Parasympathetic Activation:** Reiki often elicits deep relaxation responses, shifting the body away from states of hyperarousal. This can be especially useful during early recovery when anxiety, insomnia, and tension are common.
- **Supporting Emotional Regulation:** While not a substitute for trauma processing, Reiki may provide momentary relief from dysregulating states—offering the nervous system a brief reprieve from sympathetic overload.
- **Reinforcing Interoception:** For those disconnected from their bodies, Reiki provides a gentle entry point into somatic awareness, enabling clients to begin noticing sensation, warmth, or stillness in a safe and contained manner.

It's important to note that empirical research on Reiki's effectiveness in addiction treatment is still in its early stages. While some small studies suggest positive physiological changes, such as lowered heart rate and increased subjective well-being, the overall evidence base is limited. However, many treatment centers and trauma-informed practitioners report anecdotal success when Reiki is used in tandem with evidence-based modalities like Somatic Experiencing (SE), EMDR, or cognitive therapies.

The intention here is not to present Reiki as a cure. Still, rather as a complementary practice, a somatic doorway that helps some individuals soften their resistance to feeling, settle into their bodies, and begin to access states of calm they may not have experienced in years.

As with all somatic tools, its value lies not in mysticism but in whether the body can feel safer, even for a moment. For many in recovery, that moment marks the beginning of something life-changing.

REBUILDING SAFETY: REGULATION AS THE CORE OF RECOVERY

For many people in recovery, the hardest part isn't putting down the substance; it's staying sober when the body feels like it's constantly under threat. Long after detox, the nervous system can remain stuck in high-alert states: panic, tension, emotional flooding, or total numbness. This is the legacy of trauma, and it often goes unaddressed in traditional recovery programs.

What most people don't realize is that addiction is often a response to dysregulation, not a cause of it. Substances temporarily regulate what the nervous system cannot, slowing a racing heart, softening fear, and quieting shame. However, the nervous system still doesn't know how to return to balance when the substance is gone. That's where somatic therapy comes in.

Somatic practices help individuals learn to recognize when they are moving out of their "window of tolerance," that range of arousal where a person can think clearly, stay present, and make conscious choices. When outside that window, even small stresses can feel unbearable. Cravings can spike. Triggers hit harder. Recovery starts to feel impossible.

The goal of regulation isn't to feel calm all the time. It's about being able to *notice* when you're leaving the present moment and using tools to come back gently. These tools, like grounding through the feet, lengthening the exhale, or placing a supportive hand on the chest, aren't just coping mechanisms. They're invitations back into the body. Over time, practicing self-regulation builds trust with oneself. The body begins to learn that it doesn't have to stay stuck in survival mode forever.

This is the foundation for healing addiction at its root: not just removing the substance but restoring the ability to feel safe without it.

BUILDING EMBODIED RESILIENCE: STAYING PRESENT WITHOUT NUMBING

Early sobriety is full of moments that test your ability to stay. Stay with the feelings. Stay with the discomfort. Stay in the room when everything in your body says, *Run*. These are the moments where resilience matters, not the kind you push through with grit, but the kind that's built gently, over time, in the body.

For trauma survivors, presence itself can feel threatening. It may remind the body of past helplessness, danger, or neglect. This is why many people relapse—not because they don't want recovery, but because numbing has become a familiar form of protection.

Somatic therapies offer a different way forward: the chance to stay with emotions, sensations, and experiences *without being overwhelmed by them*. Through titration, taking on small pieces of discomfort at a time, the nervous system learns that it's safe to process what once felt overwhelming. Movement practices like trauma-sensitive yoga or Feldenkrais create space to explore what it feels like to *be in a body again*. Gentle touch, intentional breathing, and slow movement reintroduce the body to the idea of safety, not through logic, but through lived experience.

Over time, this builds what somatic therapists call embodied resilience, the ability to feel, adapt, and respond to life without having to shut down or escape. It's not about never getting triggered; it's about having the internal capacity to stay present with what arises. For someone in recovery, this can be the difference between surviving and *thriving*.

Resilience doesn't mean perfection. It means learning that you can feel pain without falling apart. That you can face discomfort without needing to numb it. That your body, once a place of chaos, can become your greatest ally in the healing process.

Chapter Summary

Somatic therapy offers something many people in recovery have never been taught: *how to be with themselves without needing to escape.* This chapter explored a range of body-based healing methods, including Somatic Experiencing and EMDR, as well as trauma-sensitive yoga and breathwork, that help restore the nervous system, reduce emotional overwhelm, and reconnect us with our physical selves.

Each approach offers its own doorway into healing. Still, all share a common purpose: to help the body release what it has held, re-regulate what has been dysregulated, and rebuild safety from the inside out. These tools are essential for those whose addiction was born out of trauma, neglect, or chronic stress. They show us that recovery is not just about abstaining; it's about learning how to *stay*, to *feel*, and to *trust the body again.*

In the next chapter, we'll explore how this somatic wisdom can be integrated into the time-tested framework of the 12 Steps. You'll see how body-based practices and nervous system awareness can deepen each step, especially for those who've long struggled with shame, dysregulation, or spiritual disconnection. Through this integration, healing becomes possible and embodied ***step by step***.

4

BEFORE THE STEPS - PREPARING THE BODY FOR RECOVERY WORK

WHY THE BODY COMES FIRST

For many in recovery, starting the 12 Steps can bring up more than just fear or doubt; it can trigger physical responses that feel overwhelming, confusing, or even paralyzing. Racing thoughts, muscle tension, shallow breathing, and emotional shutdown are not uncommon in the early stages of sobriety. These aren't just mental states but somatic indicators of a nervous system that's still on high alert.

This is why preparing the body before diving into the Steps is helpful and necessary. Without somatic readiness, even well-intentioned recovery work can feel overwhelming and too fast. When the body doesn't feel safe, the mind can't focus, and emotional healing becomes hard to reach. This chapter introduces techniques and methods aimed at rebuilding a foundation of "internal stability." This groundwork will ensure that, as you embark on the 12 Steps, you remain engaged, present, and centered throughout your journey.

Your body has been through a lot. Addiction, by nature, pulls you away from physical and emotional sensations. Substances become a way to escape discomfort but also disconnect you from your own internal guidance system. Somatic therapy helps rebuild that connection, giving your body and nervous system the support they need to re-engage with life and the Steps from a place of safety, not survival.

WHAT TRAUMA DOES TO THE NERVOUS SYSTEM

Trauma isn't always about one big event; it's about what your nervous system went through and how it adapted to survive. Whether it came from growing up in a home full of tension, experiencing sudden loss, or simply never feeling emotionally safe, trauma reshapes the way your body processes emotions and responds to stress. Over time, it can leave your nervous system stuck in patterns like fight, flight, freeze, or total shutdown.

Take Erin, for example. She didn't have a single memory she would have labeled "trauma." However, her childhood was filled with subtle yet constant stress; she was often ignored, had to walk on eggshells, and never knew when someone might explode. As an adult, Erin found herself always anxious, always braced. Alcohol gave her something that nothing else did: relief. It calmed her racing heart and let her breathe. For a little while, it felt like freedom. But it didn't last.

That's the story for many of us. Addiction becomes a coping strategy when our bodies never learned how to self-soothe. Substances give us a temporary escape from panic, numbness, or emotional overwhelm. Still, the body eventually forgets how to feel safe without them.

Understanding this changes the way we see recovery. Your cravings, your shutdowns, even your relapses, they weren't signs of failure. They were your nervous system reaching for stability the only way it knew how. That's where somatic therapy comes in. Not to rehash the past but to help your body finally process what it couldn't before.

Healing begins when you stop blaming your body and start listening to it. It's not the problem—it's been your first responder doing everything possible to keep you safe. Somatic work helps you learn how to support that system gently and with compassion so it no longer has to do it alone.

IS MY BODY READY FOR THE STEPS?

Marisol, just weeks into sobriety, attends her first 12-Step meeting. Her shoulders are tense, her face flushed, and her jaw clenched under a heavy burden of shame. When her turn to speak arrives, her mind blanks, her throat tightens, and fear freezes her in place. Shame feels like a physical threat, pushing her nervous system into a state of fight-or-flight or freeze; her heart races and her muscles lock. Her body signals "unsafe," indicating she's not yet prepared for the emotional work of the Steps.

Somatic readiness in recovery means your body has enough internal safety to feel emotions without becoming overwhelmed. It's not about being free of trauma or feeling perfect; it's about having just enough inner calm or resilience to face discomfort without panic. When the nervous system feels safe, it becomes more capable of supporting healing, emotional growth, and meaningful connection. However, for many in recovery from addiction, past trauma or chronic stress keeps the nervous system stuck in survival mode. This makes steps like the 4th and 5th, creating a moral inventory and sharing it, feel overwhelming, as they often trigger intense shame or guilt. Building somatic readiness involves cultivating enough regulation to approach these steps with stability, even when they're challenging.

Somatic readiness means you've practiced grounding techniques, such as breathing or soothing movements, enough that your body can tolerate the emotional weight of recovery work. It's not about eliminating nervousness but about having an internal anchor to stay present. You might be somatically ready if you can:

- Breathe with ease, allowing your chest and belly to move freely while keeping your body relaxed (e.g., shoulders not hunched).
- Notice and name physical sensations, like "my stomach feels tight," without shutting down completely.
- Stay in meetings or conversations, even when anxious, without an immediate urge to flee.

- Reach out for support when overwhelmed, feeling safe enough to ask for help.

You may still need support if you:

- Experience a racing heart or tightness in your chest from minor stressors, signaling the fight-or-flight response.
- Freeze, go numb or dissociate when confronted with shame or difficult emotions.
- Feel panic or overwhelm when focusing on your body or discussing your addiction.
- Frequently leave meetings early due to physical discomfort.
- Rely on substances or habits to cope with stress, indicating your nervous system doesn't yet feel safe without external crutches.

Each step in the 12-Step program offers a chance to heal, but only if your body feels safe enough to process the emotions that arise. If you identify with the "still need support" signs, that's okay. You can build readiness by practicing grounding techniques, like slow breathing or gentle movement, forming safe connections, or seeking professional guidance. These tools help stabilize your nervous system, preparing you to engage with the Steps when your body feels steadier.

SOMATIC TOOLS FOR GROUNDING AND REGULATION

Before, during, and after working through the Steps, you'll need reliable ways to stay connected to yourself, especially when things get intense.

The following tools are simple but powerful and can be practiced anywhere. These aren't exercises to perform perfectly; they're anchors to return to.

Grounding through the senses:

- Notice five things you can see, four you can touch, three you can hear, two you can smell, and one you can taste. This technique brings you into the present moment by engaging your sensory system.

Supportive self-touch:

- Place one hand on your chest and one on your belly. Feel the weight and warmth of your own presence. This gesture can calm the nervous system and re-establish a sense of containment.

Breath pacing:

- Inhale for four counts. Exhale for six. A longer exhale signals to the nervous system that it's safe to slow down.

Body scanning:

- Gently scan your body from head to toe, noticing areas of tension or relaxation without trying to fix anything. Just observe. This helps build internal awareness and track subtle changes in your nervous system.

Movement and shaking:

- Sometimes, energy needs to move. Shake out your hands or feet, stretch your spine, or walk slowly. Small movements can help discharge stress and prevent it from building into overwhelming feelings.

Incorporate these strategies as preventive measures prior to engaging in activities such as writing an inventory, making amends, or participating in meetings. They are equally beneficial in managing sudden surges of emotions. As you consistently apply these practices, they will become integrated into your internal repertoire, gradually teaching your body to recognize safety in the present moment.

SETTING UP A SOMATIC PRACTICE FOR THE STEPS AHEAD

Healing is not just about what you reflect on but also how you support yourself through the process. Setting up a simple somatic routine now can help you stay regulated and connected as you move through each of the 12 Steps.

Here are a few ways to build your own recovery-friendly somatic practice:

- **Schedule regular body check-ins.** Take 2–5 minutes daily to ask yourself: "What am I feeling in my body right now?" Let it be simple.
- **Create a physical recovery space.** Whether it's a corner of your room, a chair by the window, or a quiet spot outside, choose a place where you can breathe, write, or pause.
- **Use a transition ritual.** Before and after Step work, meetings, or emotional conversations, try using the same grounding technique to bookend your experience. This creates somatic consistency.
- **Write with the body in mind.** As you work through Steps that involve writing, pause frequently to check your body: Are your shoulders tight? Is your jaw clenched? Are your feet on the floor?
- **Be kind with pacing.** If you feel dysregulated, it's okay to pause and take a moment to regroup. Somatic work is most powerful when it's done slowly and with care.

By setting up these practices now, you'll have a reliable system of support in place as the deeper emotional work begins. You'll be able to recognize when your body needs a break when it's signaling readiness, and when it's asking for help. That's not a setback; it's part of the healing process.

If you're interested in learning more or deepening your practice, the following books offer clear, accessible guidance rooted in somatic and trauma-informed care:

The Body Keeps the Score by Bessel van der Kolk

- A foundational text on how trauma is stored in the body and why body-based healing is essential for recovery.

Waking the Tiger: Healing Trauma by Peter A. Levine

- Introduces Somatic Experiencing and explains how to release trauma from the nervous system gently.+

These resources can complement your journey through the 12 Steps by helping you build a somatic vocabulary, deepen your body awareness, and grow your personal regulation toolkit. You don't need to master them all; just begin with curiosity and care. The body will meet you where you are.

Chapter Summary

Before you begin the 12 Steps, it's essential to understand that real healing doesn't just occur in the mind; it happens in the body. Addiction leaves its imprint deep in the nervous system, and lasting recovery requires more than insight or willpower. This chapter explored how trauma shapes our physical responses, why nervous system regulation is essential, and how to recognize whether your body is truly ready for the work ahead.

You were introduced to simple, powerful somatic tools that help bring calm, awareness, and safety to recovery. These tools aren't just useful;

they're necessary. They offer a foundation of stability so that when emotions rise, memories resurface, or shame creeps in, you have a way to stay connected rather than retreat or collapse.

In the next chapter, we begin with **Step One: Admitting Powerlessness**. But this time, we'll explore what powerlessness feels like as an idea and a lived, physical experience. Together, we'll explore what happens in the body when control slips away and how recognizing those signals marks the first step in genuine, embodied recovery. You won't just read the Step. You'll feel it, and that's where the healing begins.

5

STEP ONE: IN THE BODY – ADMITTING POWERLESSNESS AS A SOMATIC SURRENDER

"We admitted we were powerless over alcohol—that our lives had become unmanageable."

THE FELT SENSE OF POWERLESSNESS

Powerlessness is not just an idea; it's a sensation your body knows intimately. Long before the mind may acknowledge the grip of addiction, the body registers it as a state of overwhelm, shutdown or collapse. You may remember moments when alcohol was no longer something you used but something that used you. In those moments, your body didn't resist; it froze. Muscles tense or go limp, and your breath shortens or disappears altogether. The body begins to say, *"I can't."*

This is not a failure of character. It is a trauma-informed survival response. The nervous system, burdened by chronic stress or unprocessed pain, shifts into a protective state. What AA names as unmanageability, the body might express as exhaustion, numbness, disconnection, or immobilization. It is the body's last-ditch effort to preserve energy when the demands of life feel too great. This is powerlessness, not in theory, but as something felt deep in the body.

Understanding this somatic reality allows for a crucial reframe: you are not weak. Your body adapted. What you felt as collapse or emotional chaos was a biological strategy to survive unbearable internal pressure. The grip of addiction, then, is not just about the substance; it's about a body locked in patterns of dysregulation, longing for relief.

Step One, in this light, becomes an act of deep listening. Admitting powerlessness is not about surrendering your dignity but honoring the truth of your body's experience. It is the first moment of coherence between what your body has been silently saying and what your spirit is finally ready to hear: *"I need help. I cannot do this alone."*

Acknowledging this truth within our bodies is not an act of surrender but rather the initial step towards healing on a somatic level.

STEP ONE IN THE FLESH: WHEN SHAME LIVES IN THE BODY

Maya sat in her car outside the meeting for twenty minutes before finally walking in. Her hands were sweating, and her jaw ached from clenching it the whole drive. She was seven days sober and already exhausted, not from withdrawals but from holding it all in. When it was her turn to speak, she wanted to say, "Hi, I'm Maya, and I'm an alcoholic." Instead, she stared at the floor and whispered, "I'm fine." Her voice barely made it out of her throat.

What froze Maya in that moment wasn't just fear. It was shame, somatic shame. The kind that doesn't live in words but in the tissues. It pulsed in her stomach, curled in her spine, and locked her voice in her throat. Her nervous system had one goal: to keep her hidden. It didn't know she was safe now. It only remembered the years she spent surviving by going into hiding.

We talk about Step One as "admitting powerlessness." Still, for many of us, our bodies admitted it long before our mouths did. Powerlessness wasn't a decision; it was a posture. Collapsed shoulders. Shallow breath. Averted eyes. It was a lifetime of trying to stay small enough not to be seen and loud enough to prove we were okay.

Addiction doesn't show up out of nowhere. It often walks in when our bodies have been on high alert for too long, buzzing with panic, dulled by depression, or frozen by fear. Substances numb what the body doesn't know how to process. That drink or drug wasn't just about pleasure; it was about survival.

Step One isn't just about saying the words. It's about letting your body say, *I can't keep doing this.* And that is no small thing. When the nervous system is used to running the show, protecting, performing, pretending, and surrendering feel dangerous. Not metaphorically. Literally.

So when shame hits like a wave, your chest tightens, your mouth dries up, your whole being wants to vanish, that's not weakness. That's your history rising to the surface. That's your body showing you just how hard it's worked to keep you alive.

And now, for the first time, it doesn't have to.

This is where Step One lives, in the moment you unclench, even just a little. In the breath you let yourself take. In the quiet, yes, that says, "I need help." That's what surrender looks like in the body. That's what courage feels like at the cellular level.

You're not failing. You're not broken. You're finally feeling.

And that means the healing has already begun.

SOMATIC ACCEPTANCE: THE FIRST STEP TOWARD REAL CHANGE

Maya didn't have a breakthrough moment. She didn't raise her hand to share in the meeting. She didn't fall to her knees in surrender. But the next morning, something small and sacred happened.

She stood alone in her kitchen, waiting for the coffee to brew. The same tightness was there in her chest, the old shame humming just beneath the surface. Her usual instinct was to distract herself: scroll her phone, busy her hands, shake it off. But this time, she stopped. She placed her hand over her heart without really thinking, and she just stood there. She noticed the tightness. The shallow breath. The lump in her throat. And for the first time in a long time, she didn't try to make it go away. She stayed.

It wasn't dramatic. It wasn't easy. But it was real. Her eyes welled up, and a single tear slipped down her cheek—not from sadness, but from the quiet relief of finally telling the truth with her body: *"This is too heavy to carry alone. I'm overwhelmed, I'm exhausted, and I don't want to keep doing it like this."*

That was the moment Maya began to taste the freedom that Step One offers, not the freedom of fixing everything, but the freedom of no longer having to pretend she had it all under control. Her body, which had spent years braced and armored, began to soften. Just a little. Just enough. Every time she paused instead of panicked, breathed instead of bolted, noticed instead of numbed, she was laying a foundation of trust within herself. Not just emotional trust, but somatic trust, the kind that lets the body know, *"We're safe now. We don't have to run."*

For Maya, Step One didn't signify a downfall; rather, it was a gradual and profound release. It involved letting go of control, shedding the need for constant performance, and moving beyond mere survival. This transformation wasn't marked by a singular moment but by a pivotal shift. This shift didn't originate in her mind but unfolded in her physical sensations: through her breath, within her chest, and down to her fingertips. It was in her body, which had long sought solace, that she finally felt a significant sense of being acknowledged and heard.

Somatic Timeline Mapping – A Nervous System Reclamation

This advanced practice introduces a visual and body-centered way of reclaiming the truth of powerlessness, not just as a concept but as a lived imprint on your body. It helps trace how chronic dysregulation, fear, or over-efforting may have shaped your nervous system long before addiction took hold.

Instructions:

1. **Draw a Horizontal Line**

On a piece of paper, draw a timeline from left (early years) to right (current day). Label key ages.

2. **Mark Moments of Powerlessness**

Using one color, mark moments where you felt helpless, afraid, or out of control, childhood incidents, traumas, emotional collapses, or even times of extreme caregiving or over-responsibility. Do not force memory; trust what your body recalls.

3. **Pause and Breathe**

After marking, pause. Notice how your body feels. Is there a temperature shift, a physical tension, or an emotional wave? Place your hand on your body where you feel it. Breathe into that space.

4. **Mark Moments of Regulation or Safety**

Using a different color, mark moments where you felt a sense of care, grounding, or safety, no matter how small. A hug. A teacher who listened. A moment with nature.

5. **Observe the Pattern**

Step back. Notice the contrast. This is your nervous system's story. You are not flawed; you have adapted. Addiction was part of a pattern of survival, not personal failure.

6. **Integrate with Compassion**

End by writing one sentence of acknowledgment to your body:

- "You did what you had to do to survive."
- "I see you now, and I'm here to stay."

Why it matters: This somatic mapping exercise honors Step One's radical honesty, accepting powerlessness not as a source of shame but as an insight. The body holds the map. You are learning how to read it, honor it, and respond with presence instead of panic.

Use this exercise once per week during Step One work or whenever old stories resurface. Over time, the nervous system becomes your ally, not your enemy. And from that truth, recovery deepens.

Chapter Summary

Step One invites us to confront a truth often felt in the body long before it's spoken aloud: that we are no longer in control. Through the lens of somatic therapy, we explored how powerlessness is not just a concept but a lived, physical experience marked by collapse, exhaustion, tension, or shutdown. These are not signs of failure but signals from a body that has been overwhelmed for too long.

By learning to recognize and respond to these signals with care rather than judgment, we begin to transform the shame of powerlessness into the wisdom of surrender. Step One, when experienced through the body, becomes an act of compassion—a quiet acknowledgment that we can't keep doing it all alone and that it's safe to stop fighting.

As we move into Step Two, we begin to explore what becomes possible when we create enough safety within to look outward again. This next step asks us to imagine that recovery is not just about breaking down but about slowly rebuilding hope, trust, and connection. For many, this is where the nervous system starts to shift from defense to openness, from collapse to curiosity.

In the next chapter, we'll explore how **Step Two: Hope** supports the body's capacity to heal when met with co-regulation, consistency, and care. This is where the groundwork laid in surrender makes space for the possibility of return.

6

STEP TWO: RECLAIMING HOPE THROUGH THE BODY, TRUSTING IN CONNECTION, SAFETY, AND SOMETHING MORE

"Came to believe that a Power greater than ourselves could restore us to sanity."

Hope doesn't always arrive like a light breaking through the clouds. Sometimes, it comes quietly, like the first full breath after a long stretch of holding it in. Step Two asks us to believe that something greater than ourselves can restore us to sanity. However, for many of us, especially in the early stages of recovery, the idea of restoration may seem distant. If Step One was about surrendering the fight, Step Two is about learning to trust again, not just in a higher power, but in our own bodies, in the safety of connection, and in the possibility that we don't have to do this alone. When your nervous system has spent years bracing, hiding, or shutting down, hope can feel dangerous. That's why Step Two begins with regulation, not just thinking our way into belief but feeling our way into possibility. Healing begins when we learn to co-regulate with others, to soften in safe spaces, and to allow our bodies to remember what it means to belong.

HOPE REQUIRES PHYSIOLOGICAL SAFETY

Hope isn't just an idea; it's something we feel. And for many in early recovery, it doesn't come easily. Hope can feel distant or even dangerous when your body has been stuck in a state of survival mode for years. Step Two invites us to believe that change is possible. Still, for that belief to take root, the body must begin to experience some sense of safety.

We don't access hope by forcing ourselves to feel it. We access it by creating conditions where it can naturally emerge through grounding, regulation, and moments of internal calm. As the body begins to soften, breathing deepens, and tension loosens, the possibility of a new future starts to feel real, both intellectually and physically.

Hope isn't about blind faith. It's about noticing even the smallest shift, a moment of stillness, a flicker of ease, a breath that feels less guarded, and letting that become evidence that something new is possible.

In recovery, this sense of safety is tangible and palpable. It's about feeling grounded, knowing you're supported physically and emotionally. This support frees your mind to entertain new ideas without fear's shadow looming. A safe body signals to the brain that dreaming, planning, and believing in greater possibilities is okay. It's not just about calming anxiety; it's about creating an environment where hope can thrive. Safety enables belief, not the other way around. By nurturing your body, you offer fertile ground for hope to grow, transforming the seemingly impossible into an achievable reality.

Hope is more than a fleeting thought; it's a state of being. It's a regulated presence that keeps you grounded amidst uncertainty. This presence is natural, unfolding when the nervous system is balanced. Safety fosters belief, not the other way around. Cultivating bodily safety allows hope to flourish, unveiling new horizons. This is where nervous system healing is crucial; nurturing your body allows hope to become a reality.

BELIEF BEGINS IN THE BODY

A few weeks into sobriety, Tasha found herself crying in the back row of a meeting. She wasn't sure why. No one had said anything especially profound, and she hadn't planned to share. But when a woman beside her reached over and gently touched her arm, Tasha's whole body exhaled. It was the first time she realized how tightly she'd been holding herself together. That moment didn't fix everything, but something in her began to soften, not in her mind, but in her body.

That's where belief begins, not as a thought but as a shift deep inside the nervous system. When your body has lived in survival mode for years, the idea of trusting anything, let alone something greater than yourself, can feel impossible. Step Two asks us to believe in the possibility of restoration, of sanity, of hope. But you can't leap into belief when your body still feels like a battlefield. That's why recovery starts not with thinking harder but with *feeling safer*.

Co-regulation is the foundation. In somatic therapy, we learn that the nervous system heals in relationship. Similar to how infants find tranquility with a consistent caregiver, adults, too, can rediscover a sense of safety by surrounding themselves with serene, encouraging individuals. In recovery, this might look like sitting in a room full of people who *get it*. It might be the way your sponsor speaks gently when you're spiraling. It might be a hug that doesn't demand anything in return. Your nervous system picks up on these signals, and slowly, sometimes for the first time, it begins to believe, *Maybe I don't have to do this alone.*

That moment is somatic. It's not about theology or dogma. It's about *sensation*. It's about the body releasing tension. The breath deepening. The chest loosening. This is what belief feels like when it's real, not recited, but received.

Step Two isn't about forcing yourself to believe in a God you can't yet define. It's about recognizing the quiet moments when something steadier begins to hold you. Maybe it's in the breath that finally comes after a panic or the warmth in your chest when someone truly sees you. That calm, that gentle grounding. It's not just emotional. It's spiritual. It's your first embodied glimpse of a Power greater than yourself. Not distant. Not theoretical. But alive within you, in your breath, your heartbeat, your ability to soften and stay. That's where faith begins: not in certainty, but in the body's quiet yes.

This is the beginning of spiritual awakening, not as a concept but as a nervous system learning what it feels like to feel safe, connected, and open to something more. A regulated body becomes the doorway to a receptive spirit. And as your body learns to settle, so too does your capacity to receive grace.

Somatic Practice: The Pendulum of Trust – Building Capacity for Hope in the Body

This practice invites the nervous system to feel into trust, not as a belief, but as a bodily experience that ebbs and flows like a pendulum. Hope becomes something you sense, not something you force.

Pendulation for Trust and Safety

1. **Create a Quiet Container**

Sit or lie down comfortably. Light a candle or use a calming object if helpful. Let your body settle. This is not about doing; it's about sensing.

2. **Find a Place of Ease**

Gently scan your body and find one area that feels *even slightly* neutral or pleasant. It could be your hands, your feet, or the air on your skin. Name that sensation: "There's warmth in my palms," or "My feet feel grounded." Stay with that for a few breaths.

3. **Touch a Place of Discomfort**

Now, shift your awareness to an area that feels tight, anxious, or numb. Stay for just 10–15 seconds. Name the sensation gently:

"There's tightness in my chest" or "My stomach feels hollow." There is no need to fix it; just notice.

4. **Return to Ease**

Go back to the place of ease. Feel it. Let your body orient again to what feels okay. This is called *pendulation*, moving between safety and stress to teach your nervous system how to return.

5. **Introduce a Phrase of Support**
    - While in your safe zone, whisper or think a phrase like:
    - "Something steadier is here."
    - "It's possible to feel held."
    - "Hope might begin in this breath."
    - Feel how your body responds to the idea of trust, even if it's tiny.
6. **End with Gentle Integration**

Place your hand over your heart or solar plexus. Say, "It's safe to not know everything right now. But I can trust this moment."

Why it matters: Step Two asks us to believe that something greater can restore us. This doesn't require immediate faith in a deity or system; it begins with your body learning how to return from overwhelm. Hope is not abstract. It's a physical capacity that can be nurtured, sensed, and expanded. Over time, these pendulum swings build a wider window of tolerance and, with it, trust in life.

A GLIMPSE OF SANITY

Elena had been sober for just over a month, but her mornings still felt like war zones. She'd wake up anxious, flooded with dread, before her feet even touched the ground. Her mind raced with panic: bills, regret, everything she'd ruined. She'd sit on the edge of her bed, fists clenched, breath shallow, bracing for the day like a soldier in a trench.

One morning, something different happened. She walked into the kitchen and, instead of grabbing her usual burnt coffee and pacing the floor, she paused. Sunlight was pouring through the window, lighting up the dust in the air. For just a moment, everything got quiet. Her shoulders dropped. Her breath deepened. She didn't think her way into it. Her body just softened. She didn't feel euphoric or healed or wise. She just felt human. Present. Safe enough to be still.

Later, she'd describe that moment as the first time she felt "okay" without reaching for something outside herself.

That's what Step Two can look like in the body. Not lightning bolts or grand revelations, but a brief, holy pause where chaos lifts and clarity enters. A flicker of sanity. A felt sense of grace. Maybe it's a kind word you didn't know you needed. Maybe it's when someone holds space for your grief without trying to fix it. Maybe it's the first time you look in the mirror and don't flinch.

As many in recovery understand, one of the most well-known definitions of insanity is "doing the same thing over and over and expecting different results." In this context, insanity is often described as returning to the drink repeatedly, even in the face of devastating consequences. But what if we looked deeper?

From a somatic perspective, what we call "insanity" might be the body stuck in a survival loop, a well-worn path of coping that once kept us alive, even if now it brings harm. These aren't just habits of thought; they're reflexes of the nervous system. They are signs of a body that hasn't yet learned another way to feel safe.

This chapter doesn't aim to redefine what you already know; it offers a new entry point. A lens that centers the body, not just the will.

When we revisit Step Two through this frame, sanity becomes more than abstinence. It becomes embodied safety. It's not just a moment of mental clarity; it's the shift when your breath deepens, your shoulders soften, and your system finds enough calm to choose a different path. It's the moment your body tells the truth before your mind can explain it.

You don't need to dissect that moment to believe in it. You just need to feel it. That flicker of nervous system steadiness is where the miracle begins. That's the sanity we're inviting back, one pause, one breath, one embodied choice at a time.

Chapter Summary

Step Two is where the tide begins to turn, not through logic or willpower but through the nervous system's first glimpse of safety. From a somatic perspective, believing in a Power greater than ourselves isn't just a mental leap; it's a felt shift inside the body. It's the moment you exhale without realizing. It's when someone looks at you with compassion, and your guard drops, even for a second. It's when the chaos quiets, not because life is fixed, but because something steadier has entered the room.

For alcoholics, the insanity isn't just in drinking again; it's in believing we can outrun pain alone. Step Two offers a radical alternative: the embodied possibility that we don't have to do this by ourselves. And that belief is born not in theology but in the nervous system's ability to co-regulate, to soften, to feel connected and seen. Through those micro-moments of calm, our bodies begin to remember what sanity feels like, not perfection, but presence. Not escape, but safety.

In this chapter, we explored how the body begins to trust again through gentle contact, safe relationships, and soothing environments. We repeated signals that it's okay to stop bracing. Step Two is the nervous system's whisper: *maybe I'm not beyond help.* It's not a certainty; it's a possibility. And the possibility is the beginning of a transformation.

In the next chapter, we'll move deeper into that process. **Step Three - Letting Go** isn't about giving up, but letting go in the body. It's where control, tension, and survival start to give way to trust, softening, and surrender. And it's where the body, once frozen by fear, begins to make space for something new to take root.

7

STEP THREE: LETTING GO OF CONTROL AS A PHYSICAL PRACTICE

"Made a decision to turn our will and our lives over to the care of God as we understood Him."

SURRENDER IS A FELT EXPERIENCE

Surrender might be one of the most misinterpreted words in recovery. We hear it and think, "giving up." But for many of us, especially those who've lived through trauma, betrayal, or long-term chaos, surrender never felt safe. It felt like exposure. Letting go meant being vulnerable in dangerous places. So, we learned to grip tightly. To stay sharp. To stay in control. Because somewhere along the way, control became our safety net.

Then comes Step Three, asking us to turn our will and our lives over to something greater. But what if you don't believe in God? Or worse, what if God, or the people who claimed to speak for Him, were part of your trauma?

This is where many freeze. Not because they're unwilling but because their body still lives in survival mode. You might sit in a meeting and hear someone say, "just turn it over," and feel your chest tighten, your jaw lock, your thoughts race. That's not rebellion. That's your nervous system saying, *I've been here before, and I got hurt.*

Jonah, newly sober and quietly skeptical of everything "spiritual," said it best: "Every time someone said 'just let go,' I clenched harder. My whole body would go on high alert." He wasn't resisting the program. His body was protecting him like it always had.

That's why real surrender doesn't start in the mind. It starts in the body. Somatic therapy teaches us this: you can't force safety. You create it. A deep breath that doesn't feel rushed. A moment of stillness that doesn't trigger panic. A softening in the belly. These aren't just signs of calm; they're the beginning of surrender.

And surrender, in this context, isn't about kneeling at an altar. It's about giving yourself permission to stop fighting. Not because you've been defeated, but because, for the first time, you're safe enough to put the armor down.

Step Three isn't asking us to believe in someone else's God. It's asking us to trust that we no longer have to carry it alone. That's surrender. Not a fall, but a soft landing.

WHEN LETTING GO FEELS LIKE LOSING CONTROL

Somewhere along our journey, we adopted the notion that maintaining control was equivalent to ensuring our safety. We meticulously managed every aspect of our existence, including our environment, emotional landscape, public persona, and even our deepest pains. In essence, control morphed into a form of unwavering faith for us. Thus, when we encounter Step Three's invitation to relinquish control, our physiological response isn't automatically one of compliance. Instead, our bodies often recoil, haunted by memories of past betrayals and disappointments, questioning, *Are you sure? The last time you placed your trust in something, it ended in anguish.*

This reaction isn't indicative of a flaw; it's a testament to our innate survival mechanisms.

Consider Jonah's narrative, for example. As he navigated through his fourth month of sobriety, he found himself grappling with the essence of Step Three. It wasn't just the religious undertones that unsettled him; it was more about his visceral reactions to attempts at relaxation. *"Each time I would attempt to lie down and focus on my breathing,"* he recounted, *"my chest would constrict, as if preparing to withstand an assault. It was a revelation for me, I had never experienced a sense of true safety in my life."*

Jonah's journey through somatic exercises didn't involve a forceful quest for surrender. Instead, he cultivated an awareness of his body's signals: the superficiality of his breath, the unconscious clenching of his fists, the perpetual tension in his shoulders. His path to peace wasn't paved with prayers. Still, it was instead a gradual process of observation and acknowledgment, breath by breath, relaxation by relaxation, moment by moment. This was how he embodied Step Three. The act of letting go transcends spiritual enlightenment; it represents the initial steps towards rebuilding trust within one's body, even if it's just a semblance of trust.

Your concept of a higher power might diverge from traditional notions. It could be found within the fellowship, through music, amidst the tranquility of nature, or simply in the act of breathing. This is significant. This matters. The Big Book's phrasing, "as we understood Him," underscores a pivotal truth: recovery isn't contingent upon conforming to someone else's spiritual convictions. It's about acknowledging our limitations in shouldering life's burdens alone and embracing a collective or internal strength.

Step Three is less about coercing trust and more about fostering an environment where trust can naturally emerge. It's a process characterized by yielding, not yielding control, by attuning to the body's needs, not disregarding them. It invites our nervous system to experience, perhaps for the first time, a state of non-resistance—a signal that it's finally safe to cease the endless battle. True surrender doesn't signify defeat. It represents a profound transformation, not a gesture of giving up, but a powerful act of reclaiming one's self.

MY STORY: TURNING IT OVER, MY WAY

I didn't walk into recovery with a white-light moment. I didn't fall to my knees or cry out to God. In fact, I wasn't even sure what I believed, just that I couldn't keep living the way I was. I had been drinking alcoholically for about ten years. There were so many attempts to quit, so many detoxes, I lost count. I went through three rehabs, convinced each time I'd finally found the answer, only to fall again. I didn't lose my family, but I came close to losing myself.

The word "God" made me uncomfortable. It still does, sometimes. I heard it in meetings, saw it printed on the Steps, and felt like I was doing something wrong because I didn't believe. But I kept coming back. I kept listening. And I started to understand that Step Three didn't require me to believe in someone else's version of God. It asked me to stop doing it all my way. *To turn my will and my life over to something greater than my chaos.*

For me, that "greater" wasn't God in the traditional sense. It was stillness. It was Reiki, the warmth in my hands during a quiet session. It was breath; deep, grounding, and slow. It was the calming space of meditation, where I could hear something inside me that wasn't fear. That's what I turn my life over to now — a deeper awareness, a quiet current of peace that I can actually feel.

And most importantly, it was my sponsor. A woman who never judged me for slipping. Who didn't flinch when I cried, doubted, or said, *"I'm not sure I can do this."* She sat with me when I wanted to run. She reminded me that surrender doesn't have to look dramatic; sometimes it just means showing up one more time, without pretending. This book is for her and for every sponsor who's sat with someone in the dark and waited until they could see again.

Step Three is still unfolding for me. I haven't mastered it, but I've come to understand that surrender isn't a leap, it's a slow return.

Through somatic practices, Reiki, and quiet moments in meditation, I've learned how to feel my way back into my body, back into presence. I breathe. I ground. I soften. I let go a little more each day. And in those moments, I don't feel lost, I feel like myself. That's the kind of surrender I can live with. That's the kind that keeps me coming back.

Reflection Section: *Breath as Your Anchor*

Settle into a safe space.

- Find a quiet, undisturbed environment where you can sit or lie down comfortably. Allow your body to relax without the need to "do" anything.

Notice your contact with the ground.

- Feel where your body connects with the surface beneath you, your feet on the floor, your back against a chair, your hips grounded. Let gravity support you. Say silently, *"I am supported."*

Breathe to regulate your nervous system.

- Inhale through your nose for a count of **4** (fill your belly).
- Hold briefly at the top.
- Exhale slowly through your mouth for a count of **6** (like a gentle sigh).
- Repeat for **3–5 full rounds**, lengthening the exhale slightly each time.

Engage heart-body awareness.

- Place one hand over your heart and the other on your belly. Notice any movement with each breath. This gesture reminds your system that you are safe and present.

Whisper or affirm with intention.

Speak gently to your body:

- *"It's safe to let go."*
- *"I am not alone."*
- *"I don't have to hold it all anymore."*

Scan for tension with compassion.

- Slowly move your awareness from head to toe. Notice if you're holding tension (jaw, shoulders, chest, stomach). Invite those areas to soften, not forcefully, but with kindness.

Stay present for a few more breaths.

- Just be. Let the moment hold you. No need to analyze or achieve anything. Simply notice how surrender *feels*, not as giving up, but as giving into safety.

Prayer for Embodied Surrender

Higher Power,

I release the weight I've been carrying, the need to control, to fix, to fight.

Help me feel Your care not just in thought, but in my body, breath, and bones.

Let my surrender be a returning-

to peace, to presence, to the truth that I am already held.

Teach me to trust from the inside out.

When fear tightens its grip, anchor me in safety.

When I forget how to let go, remind me, you never let go of me.

Amen.

"Surrender is not weakness—it is my nervous system learning to trust again. I am safe to let go. I am held. I am healing."

Chapter Summary

Step Three isn't just a spiritual concept; it's a full-body experience. In this chapter, we explored surrender not as defeat, but as the slow, embodied shift from bracing to trusting. For many of us, especially those who've lived through trauma or carry distrust toward the word "God," the idea of turning our will over can feel impossible. But somatic healing reframes surrender: not as something we force, but something that arises naturally when the body begins to feel safe.

We saw how control often masquerades as protection, how the tension in our jaw, the clench in our fists, the shallow breath aren't flaws, but signals that our nervous system is still in survival mode. And we learned that real surrender begins with noticing: a breath that deepens, a muscle that softens, a moment where the body realizes it doesn't have to grip so tightly. In that space, trust begins to take root.

Step Four asks us to turn inward, not to punish ourselves or relive the past, but to gently uncover the stories we've been carrying in our bodies. Through a somatic lens, inventory becomes less about judgment and more about integration. We're not here to bulldoze through trauma, but to approach it with care, regulation, and respect. In the next chapter, we'll explore how to revisit our past in a way that honors the truth of what happened and honors the body that kept us alive through it all.

8

STEPS FOUR: REVISITING THE PAST SOMATICALLY

"Made a searching and fearless moral inventory of ourselves."

EMOTIONAL INVENTORY CAN TRIGGER TRAUMA RESPONSES

Step Four asks us to take a fearless moral inventory, to look back at our past with honesty and depth. But for many, this process can feel like staring into a mirror that doesn't just reflect the surface, but reveals the raw, tangled emotional landscape underneath. It's not just about what we did, it's about what shaped us, what we learned to hide, and what we were never allowed to feel. And for that reason, this step often awakens more than memory; it awakens the body.

Take Lila, for example. Six months into sobriety, she sat down to write her first inventory. She lit a candle, opened her notebook, and froze. Her heart began to race. Her hands trembled. She couldn't remember what she was supposed to write, only that she suddenly felt ten years old again, alone in her bedroom, trying not to cry too loudly after another one of her dad's outbursts. Lila wasn't resisting the work. Her body was remembering what it had to forget to survive.

This is the part of Step Four no one warns you about. You might notice your chest tightening, your breath growing shallow, or your stomach turning to knots. You might find yourself suddenly exhausted, irritable, or numb. These are not signs of failure. They are your body's way of bracing for impact. When the nervous system perceives danger, real or remembered, it activates defenses like fight, flight, freeze, or collapse. This isn't rebellion. It's protection.

These responses are deeply ingrained and often unconscious. And they're not there to derail your recovery, they're evidence that your body is participating. That it's alert. That it's trying to keep you safe, even if the threat is no longer present. Step Four, approached somatically, becomes a practice not just of writing your history, but of tending to the body that lived through it.

This is why awareness is essential. When you recognize that overwhelming emotions, shutdown, or physical discomfort are part of the process, not something to be ashamed of, you can meet them with care instead of judgment. You can pause. Breathe. Take breaks. You can move through inventory at your own pace, not the pace of urgency or pressure.

Step Four isn't about re-traumatizing yourself. It's about reclaiming your truth safely. It's about walking through the past, not to stay there, but to loosen its grip on your body. When done with somatic awareness, inventory becomes more than reflection, it becomes release. And every time you stay present, even for a moment longer than before, you're breaking the cycle of fear and beginning the work of embodied healing.

LISTENING TO THE BODY'S VERSION OF THE STORY

Step Four asks us to take a searching and fearless moral inventory, but what often goes unspoken is that the body has been keeping its own version of the story. The body remembers long before we write a word, not in thoughts or timelines, but in clenched shoulders, restless legs, tight throats, and the pressure behind our eyes. The inventory isn't just about what happened, it's about how we carried it, how we survived it, and what it's still costing us to hold it in.

Many of us brace for Step Four like we're about to dive into a burning house. But it doesn't have to be that way. What if instead of rushing toward every painful memory, we slowed down and let the body lead? What if we treated every tension, every discomfort, every urge to flee not as resistance, but as intelligence? The body isn't trying to stop you from healing, it's asking to be included. Inventory, from a somatic perspective, isn't about dissecting pain. It's about giving it space. Sometimes the most honest thing we can do is pause, breathe, and ask our body, *What part of this story still lives in me?*

When Lila sat down to write her Fourth Step, she expected it to be hard, but she didn't expect her entire body to rebel. Her hands trembled before they even touched the page. Her vision blurred. Her chest tightened like a vice, and her stomach churned with nausea. She hadn't even written a word yet. When she thought about the relationships she'd damaged, the betrayals, the lies, the nights she disappeared, a voice rose in her head, sharp and familiar: *"You ruined everything. You always ruin everything."* It was her mother's voice. It came with a rush of heat in her face and a shaking in her legs.

At first, Lila thought something was wrong with her, that she was too broken to face the truth. She kept saying, "I guess I'm just not ready." But then her sponsor suggested something different: *"What if your body's not stopping you — what if it's showing you the path?"*

So Lila tried again. This time, she wrote just one sentence. Then she stopped. She pressed her feet into the floor. She let herself notice the knot in her throat without trying to swallow it down. When her breath got shallow, she didn't panic. She stayed. And when the tears came, she let them. No judgment. No rushing. Just space.

Little by little, she returned to the page, not with force, but with care. She wasn't powering through her inventory but partnering with her body to write it. And something shifted. What once felt like a breakdown started to feel like a breakthrough. The shame didn't vanish, but it softened. Her body stopped running. And for the first time, she realized she wasn't just remembering the past, she was letting it go.

Lila's experience is not unique; many of us find that when we begin to write about harm, our body speaks louder than our words. Sometimes it screams. And sometimes it just whispers *not yet*. In early recovery, we may think we need to power through. Push harder. "Do the work." But somatic wisdom invites us to slow down. To listen. To understand that deep self-inquiry is not just emotional, it's biological.

The body holds timelines of its own. A memory written down at 10 a.m. may echo like it happened to your nervous system five minutes ago. That's why it's not about *how much* you can write in a day, it's about *how fully you can stay with yourself* while doing it. Even stopping to stretch, hum, or press your feet to the floor can anchor you more deeply than pushing through another paragraph. These simple acts are not distractions from the work; they *are* the work.

There's no prize for speed here. What matters is presence. When you pause, when you regulate, when you give your nervous system a chance to catch up with your courage, that's where true integration happens. That's where shame begins to loosen its grip. Not because we've out-thought it, but because we've out-held it.

Step Four becomes transformative not through the inventory itself but through how we relate to it. With softness. With pacing. With the understanding that we are building capacity, not reliving trauma. That every moment we stay present with what once overwhelmed us is a quiet act of reclamation.

Eventually, you'll look back and realize you didn't just make a list. You made space. Space for your story. Space for your truth. Space for your body to no longer be the battleground where the past and present collide, but instead, the ground where healing finally takes root.

SOMATIC PRACTICE: INVENTORY WALK – RELEASING SHADOWS WITH THE EARTH

This practice invites you to take your Step Four inventory outdoors, into nature where your body can move, breathe, and process without the confines of a room. By walking in a natural space, you allow the land to hold your reflections and the rhythm of your steps to metabolize your emotions. This practice draws on ecotherapy and somatic tracking principles, utilizing nature as a co-regulator for addressing shame, grief, and unresolved emotional wounds.

Instructions:

Choose a Natural Path

- Find a safe, quiet outdoor place: a forest trail, beach, park path, or even a quiet residential sidewalk lined with trees. The key is having space where you can walk without interruption for 20–30 minutes.

Set an Intention Before You Begin

- Pause before starting. Place one hand on your heart, one on your belly. Whisper: *"As I walk, I allow what needs to arise to come. I will meet it with breath, not blame."*

Carry a Pocket Stone or Object

- Choose a small natural object (like a stone, leaf, or stick) to carry. This will become your "inventory stone." Let it symbolize what you are willing to face today, just one memory, pattern, or truth.

Begin Walking with Breath Awareness

- Let your breath match your steps. Inhale for 3–4 steps, exhale for 4–6. You're not rushing or solving, just staying with yourself. As emotions arise, let them move through your body as sensation, not story.

Name What Comes – Quietly or in a Whisper

- As you walk, name internal experiences softly: "anger," "betrayal," "I judged her," "I was scared." No fixing. Just naming and walking. Your body will begin to release what it's ready to.

Pause and Ground Midway

- Halfway through, stop and place your stone on the earth. You can bury it slightly, leave it under a tree, or simply set it down. Say: *"I leave this story here for now. The earth can hold it with me."*
- This is not about dumping emotion but **co-holding** it in a larger container, nature's nervous system.

Return with a Word of Integration

- On your walk back, choose one word you want to walk with today: "truth," "forgiveness," "release," "witness." Allow your body to start feeling that word as an embodied state.

Close with Physical Touch

- When you finish, press your hands to your thighs or chest and whisper: *"I walked through part of my past today. And I stayed with myself."*

Why This Practice Is Powerful:

- Movement metabolizes trauma.
- Nature regulates the nervous system and invites humility without shame.

- The act of leaving the object behind builds a physical ritual of release.

Step Four becomes not just a written moral inventory, but a **lived act of truth-telling** in motion.

STAYING PRESENT WHEN THE PAST ARISES

By now, you've likely unearthed memories that don't just knock, they barge in. Some come fast, others creep in sideways. But either way, the question isn't *what happened then?* It's *what do I choose to do now?* Because Step Four isn't about drowning in the past, it's about reclaiming your presence within it.

Staying present doesn't mean becoming immune to pain. It means you've learned how to meet it differently. You're not dissociating. You're not running. You're not clinging to the old story. You're standing, maybe shaking, crying, maybe breathing heavy, but still *here*. That is power. That is healing.

In somatic recovery, presence is a muscle. You don't need to be fearless to face your inventory. You need to be willing to feel what's true without abandoning yourself. That might mean writing a little, then resting. It might mean crying without explanation. It might mean putting your hand on your heart and saying: *I'm still here. And I'm not going anywhere.*

This is the real gift of Step Four: not just that we remember, but that we return to the body, to the breath, to the moment. With every act of self-staying, we undo the belief that our past defines us. What defines us now is how we *remain*. Honest. Grounded. Present.

You don't walk out of this step lighter because you've escaped your past. You walk out stronger because you *face it without leaving yourself behind*.

Chapter Summary

Step Four asked us to take a searching and fearless moral inventory, but this time, we approached it through the body, not just the mind. As we unearthed the memories, patterns, and harm of the past, we noticed how those experiences didn't just live in words; they lived in muscle tension, breath patterns, and emotional reflexes that shaped how we moved through the world.

This step wasn't about judgment. It was about witnessing. It was about meeting the parts of ourselves we've hidden or pushed away, and learning to stay present with what arises, without shutting down. By slowing down and listening to our bodies, we allowed ourselves to face the truth safely, at our own pace, and with compassion instead of shame.

Now we step into **Step Five**, not just to tell our story, but to *liberate* it from the silence it's lived in. This is more than confession. This is exhale. This is the moment when truth is no longer confined to the body. Where what was once buried in shame begins to rise, not to haunt us, but to be held, witnessed, and finally released. In the next chapter, we'll explore how speaking the truth out loud, in the presence of safety, support, and grounded compassion, becomes the turning point where we stop carrying the past alone.

9

STEP FIVE: FEELING THE PAST TO FINALLY RELEASE IT

"Admitted to God, to ourselves, and to another human being the exact nature of our wrongs."

STEP FIVE BECOMES A NERVOUS SYSTEM RELEASE

In recovery, Step Five offers more than emotional catharsis; it is a vital release for the nervous system. When you share your deepest truths with another, it is not just words that leave your lips; it is a cascade of pent-up tension and shame that exits your body. This act of confiding becomes a powerful tool for emotional relief and regulation. It allows the nervous system to shift from hypervigilance to calm, easing the burden of carrying secrets alone.

Being seen and heard by another person can soothe the primal instincts that keep you on edge. When someone listens without judgment, it creates a safe space where your survival responses can relax. The very act of being acknowledged validates your experiences, allowing your body to find equilibrium. It is as if the weight of silence lifts, replaced by the comfort of connection and understanding. In these moments, your nervous system finds solace in the shared human experience, leading to a profound sense of relief.

Step Five also facilitates the release of stored shame. Shame's insidious grip can keep you trapped in a cycle of self-reproach and isolation. By vocalizing these feelings, you break its hold, allowing your body to breathe freely again. This release is not only physical but also emotional and spiritual. It is like a heavy cloak is removed, revealing a lighter, more authentic self beneath. This liberation transcends mere words, touching every facet of your being.

CONFESSION AS A FULL-BODY SURRENDER

Step Five is more than a checkpoint in recovery. It's a reckoning. A rebirth. The moment where silence ends, not just in words, but in the *body*. We're asked to admit "to God, to ourselves, and to another human being the exact nature of our wrongs." But this isn't just about speaking. It's about *freeing ourselves from the weight of what we've carried in secret for far too long.*

In somatic healing, the body is not a passive witness to our story, it *is* the story. The body holds what the mind hides. Every unfinished sentence. Every swallowed apology. Every time we told ourselves *it wasn't that bad.* The jaw remembers what we couldn't say. The gut holds what we couldn't face. The breath shortens when shame walks in.

Step Five is not just confession, it's exorcism.

This is where relapse often loses its grip. Why? Because the truth no longer lives in isolation. Because shame can't survive in the light. Because saying it out loud, in the presence of another human being who doesn't flinch, who stays, tells the nervous system something it's never known: *I can tell the truth and still belong.*

For many of us, it's the first time we've spoken without performance. Without armor. Without the desperate need to control how we're seen. And in that raw, trembling honesty, something breaks open. The tears we swore we'd never cry fall freely. The breath finally deepens. The weight doesn't just lift, it *moves*. It *leaves*.

When approached somatically, Step Five becomes a ritual of release, not a mental exercise, not a guilt-dump, not a forced performance of remorse. It's a *return* to the voice, to the breath, to the body we abandoned in order to survive. It's where we stop narrating our pain like a distant story and start letting it *leave the body*.

In somatic therapy, we learn that the body holds the residue of our unspoken truths, in our fascia, our breath patterns, our nervous system's fight-or-flight reflexes. We learn to notice, feel, and stay with the physical sensations that arise when we speak what we once buried. A lump in the throat isn't just discomfort; it's a signal. A tremble in the hands isn't weakness; it's movement. These are the body's ways of saying, *Something is being released.* When we include the body in confession, we don't just say what happened; we *let it go*, cell by cell, breath by breath.

This is the heart of Step Five through a somatic lens: the merging of truth with presence. It's not about how well we articulate. It's about how *deeply we inhabit* what we're finally ready to say and how gently we allow it to move through and out of us.

There is no script. There is only honesty and the willingness to stay present through the heat, the shaking, the tears, the pauses. This is what transformation sounds like. What it *feels* like. It's not clean. It's not pretty. But it's *real*.

And it's in that raw realness when the truth is finally spoken through lips that used to tremble that healing rushes in.

WHERE THE BODY SPEAKS: WALKING OUT WHAT WAS BURIED

A Somatic Approach to Step Five

Step Five is not just a step of spoken truth; it's a step of somatic release. After carrying secrets in the body for years, this is your opportunity to *let go with your whole being*. And to do that, the *environment* and the *presence of another* matter deeply. Somatic healing teaches us that safety isn't just an idea; it's something the *nervous system needs to feel*. That's why movement, nature, and relational safety can transform your Fifth Step into a full-body experience of liberation.

Why Nature and Movement Support Step Five Somatically:

- **Open spaces** like the beach or woods down-regulate the nervous system. The natural world doesn't demand anything from you, it allows you just to be. This calms the threat response that might otherwise surface during vulnerable sharing.
- **Bilateral movement** (like walking) activates both hemispheres of the brain, which helps you process emotional material with greater balance and clarity. It keeps the body from locking up in a freeze.
- **Rhythmic walking** provides the body with a soothing, repetitive pattern, a kind of *neural lullaby*, that creates internal stability, even as you're expressing unstable or painful truths.
- **Safe companionship** co-regulates the nervous system. A sponsor or trusted person who listens with presence and non-judgment becomes a *regulating anchor*, their calm signals safety to your body.
- **Sensory grounding** from the earth beneath your feet, the wind on your skin, the sound of water, all pull you *out of mental spirals and into the present moment*, which is essential when navigating shame or trauma memory.
- **Silence between words** gives the body space to process. Somatic release isn't always verbal; sometimes the biggest shift happens in the quiet, in the sigh that follows the truth being spoken.

How to Prepare for a Step Five Walk

- **Choose the right person.** Someone who can hold emotional space without rushing to fix. Their nervous system will help regulate yours; this is an example of somatic co-regulation in action.
- **Pick a place with natural rhythm.** Beaches, forest trails, lake paths; places that breathe with you. Nature naturally lowers cortisol and softens hypervigilance.
- **Set your intention.** You're not performing. You're not being judged. You're releasing. Let your body *know* that.
- **Let movement lead.** Walk slowly. Let your steps support your speech. If the story is hard, let the body move it through.
- **Feel your feet.** Grounding is not just a metaphor. The pressure of your feet against the earth sends safety signals to the brainstem. This is somatic containment.
- **Pause often.** Let yourself stop when needed. Rest your hand on your chest or belly. Regulate. Breathe. There's no rush. Each pause is a kindness to your system.
- **Close with a gesture of release.** When you've shared what needs to be shared, let it go with intention: throw a stone, touch the ocean, say a simple phrase like, *"This no longer lives in me."*

Final Somatic Reminder

The body heals through experience, not explanation. Step Five is not about saying the perfect thing; it's about letting what's been buried come to the surface *safely*. When you combine movement, nature, and trusted connection, you're not just telling your story, you're reclaiming it with every step.

Let the earth carry what the body no longer needs to hold.

Chapter Summary

Step Five takes on new significance here. Sharing your experiences with another can bring profound relief. When another person listens without judgment, it allows your nervous system to shift from defense to ease. This act of being seen and heard not only calms survival responses but also facilitates a release of stored shame. It's a liberation that spans the physical, emotional, and spiritual dimensions of self.

As we conclude this segment of our journey, let us reflect on Step Five's profound opportunity for transformation. This step is not merely a milestone but a gateway to deeper healing and self-discovery. By approaching this phase with openness and vulnerability, you allow yourself to engage with your recovery more meaningfully.

In embracing Step Five, you acknowledge your past behaviors and their impacts and set the groundwork for true change. This step challenges you to confront your vulnerabilities and fears, yet growth blooms in this confrontation.

As we move into **Step Six**, the journey turns inward once again, this time to face the traits and protective patterns we've begun to see more clearly. This next chapter isn't about force or perfection; it's about becoming willing. Willing to release the defenses that once served us but now keep us bound. Step Six asks us to stand at the edge of change, not with shame, but with curiosity and courage. It invites us to let go, not all at once, but as the body becomes ready, so that healing can move beyond awareness and into transformation.

10

STEP SIX: RELEASING DEFENSES, NOT JUST DEFECTS

"Were entirely ready to have God remove all these defects of character."

CHARACTER DEFECTS AS PROTECTIVE ADAPTATIONS

Imagine standing at a crossroads, where each path represents a choice between holding onto old habits and embracing change. At this juncture, your so-called "character defects" may appear as obstacles. Yet, they often originate from a place of self-protection. These behaviors, labeled as defects, once served as survival strategies during turbulent times. They were never mere flaws but adaptations that helped you navigate unsafe environments. They offered a semblance of control and safety in an unpredictable world.

Releasing these adaptations demands compassion, not punishment. It begins with understanding their origins, which softens the harsh inner critic that often accompanies self-reflection. Consider a child who learns to be invisible to avoid conflict at home; this behavior, while a defect in adulthood, was once a shield. Recognizing this transforms judgment into empathy. You begin to see these traits not as personal failures but as remnants of past battles fought and survived.

To release these defenses, approach them with curiosity and kindness, allowing for gradual change. I'd like you to reflect on how these behaviors once served you and how they might now hinder your growth. This understanding invites transformation, not through force but through acceptance. By acknowledging the protective role these adaptations played, you open the door to healing and growth.

THE NERVOUS SYSTEM DEFENDS AGAINST PAST HARM

Step Six invites us to become ready, not to fix ourselves or force transformation, but to open ourselves to the possibility of change. Yet readiness isn't just a decision made in the mind. It must also be felt and supported in the body. And for many of us, the body isn't ready. Not because it's broken or resistant but because it's still protecting us from the pain that once felt unbearable.

When we encounter stress or threat, whether physical, emotional, or relational, the body reacts. It doesn't wait for permission or analysis. It prepares to defend. This can show up in many ways: anger, tension, withdrawal, perfectionism, people-pleasing, addiction, or emotional numbness. These aren't moral defects; they are protective patterns that once helped us survive unsafe or unpredictable situations.

By the time we arrive at Step Six, we often begin to see how these patterns no longer serve us. We may feel exhausted by our need to stay in control, ashamed of how we lash out, or defeated by our emotional shutdowns. But it's important to remember: these habits didn't start as flaws. They started as protection.

The challenge of Step Six is that it asks us to become willing to let go of these defenses. But the body may not yet believe it's safe to do so. A quick temper might have protected us from feeling powerless. Numbing may have buffered us from grief. Perfectionism might have helped us avoid rejection. These traits are not random; they were formed for a reason.

So when we ask, *"Am I entirely ready to let this go?"* we must include the body in that question. Because if the body is still bracing for harm, it will hold on. Not out of defiance but out of loyalty to what once kept us safe.

Readiness, then, is not about pressure; it's about permission. It's about letting the body know: *You're safe now. You don't have to keep doing this.* It's about gently and gradually relaxing the very systems that once had to stay on guard. This kind of readiness grows slowly through consistency, compassion, and listening, not just to our thoughts but to the cues in our breath, posture, and inner sensations.

Step Six becomes a quiet conversation between mind and body: *I am willing to live without this armor... when I feel safe enough to put it down.* And that safety may need to be rebuilt again and again. Each time we respond instead of react, breathe instead of brace, feel instead of flee, we teach the body that it no longer has to live in the past.

This work isn't about perfection. It isn't about force. It's about willingness, a slow, steady willingness to trust that change is possible and that who we are beneath our defenses has been there all along, waiting for the chance to emerge and breathe freely again.

SOMATIC PRACTICE: WATER RELEASE RITUAL – SURRENDERING OLD SURVIVAL STRATEGIES

Overview:

Step Six asks us to become *entirely ready* to let go of the character traits and survival strategies that no longer serve us. But readiness doesn't come from the mind alone; it emerges from the body. This practice utilizes running water as a co-regulator to support the release of old emotional armor, including shame, defensiveness, self-judgment, or the need for control.

Instructions:

Find a Flowing Water Source

- This could be a shower, bath, stream, sink, or even a bowl of water. What matters is *movement*. Water mirrors your intention to allow, cleanse, and surrender.

Choose One Trait or Pattern

- Stand or sit quietly for a moment. Bring to mind one character trait, a survival pattern, that feels ready to soften. Say its name out loud or in your heart (e.g., "perfectionism," "rage," "people-pleasing").

Activate Physical Movement

- Let your hands rub together vigorously. Feel heat. Then, touch your chest, arms, or jaw, wherever that trait tends to live in your body. Breathe into that area. You are waking up old tension so it can leave.

Engage with the Water

- Place your hands under the flowing water. Imagine this water moving through you, reaching places where that trait once lived. Speak aloud (or silently):

"You kept me safe when I didn't know how."

"You don't have to protect me anymore."

"I am ready to soften."

Shake, Stretch, or Sigh

- Let your body respond. Shake out your arms, twist your torso, yawn, and exhale audibly. These are signs the nervous system is resetting. Let the old energy move *through* and *out*.

Close with a Somatic Intention

- Dry off or step away from the water. Press your feet into the ground and say: *"I am becoming ready. My body is learning to release."*
- Place a hand over your heart and anchor this new state with a deep breath.

Why It Works:

- Water offers symbolic and sensory release. It mimics the flow of letting go.
- The body learns *readiness* through movement, not analysis.
- Rather than labeling traits as "defects," this honors them as strategies that once ensured survival.

It makes Step Six not about *fixing* but about *flowing forward* with less armor.

BECOMING READY, ONE BREATH AT A TIME

Step Six doesn't demand that we be perfect, pure, or entirely healed. It simply asks us to be willing, willing to consider the possibility that the patterns we've leaned on to survive may no longer serve who we're becoming. It is not a test of strength or self-discipline but a quiet invitation to meet ourselves right where we are, with honesty and compassion.

For many of us, the behaviors we hope to release weren't born of moral failure; they were born of fear, pain, and the deep wisdom of the body trying to keep us safe. These aren't just psychological patterns; they are somatic memories encoded into the way we breathe, speak, react, and relate. To release them, we must do more than wish them away. We must learn how to feel safe enough to let them go.

And that takes time.

Becoming "entirely ready" is not about arriving at a flawless mindset. It's about moving toward the nervous system's *readiness to trust again*, to soften, to feel, and to surrender its protective armor in exchange for something more life-giving. Sometimes, that readiness shows up in small moments: a softened jaw during a hard conversation, a willingness to pause before reacting, a breath held a little less tightly in the chest.

This is the sacred work of Step Six, not dramatic transformation overnight, but a steady willingness to make space for change. A space where the nervous system is met, not pushed. Where we stop fighting ourselves and begin listening.

One layer at a time. One moment at a time. One breath at a time.

Higher Power,

I am willing to release what no longer serves me,

but I also honor what once protected me.

Help me meet my patterns with compassion,

not shame.

Help me soften the parts of me that still brace for harm.

I don't need to force healing—

I only need to allow it.

Show me how to trust the slow work of becoming ready.

Teach my body it is safe now to let go.

One breath at a time,

one layer at a time,

I welcome the change You are making in me.

Amen.

"I am becoming ready. My body is learning to feel safe without the patterns that once protected me. I do not rush my healing—I trust its rhythm."

Chapter Summary

Step Six asks us to become entirely ready to have our patterns, our so-called defects, removed. But readiness isn't about trying harder. It's about allowing the body to loosen its grip on what once felt necessary. Many of the behaviors we wish to change didn't begin as flaws; they began as survival responses. Control, rage, people-pleasing, perfectionism, or emotional disconnection may have once protected us from pain or rejection.

This chapter reminded us that the body must feel safe before releasing what it once needed to survive. Readiness is not a mental decision alone; it's a slow, somatic unfolding. Each time we meet these old patterns with curiosity instead of shame, we create space for real transformation. We learn that we don't need to force change; we need to *support* it.

As we move into **Step Seven**, the focus shifts from readiness to release. But what does it actually mean to let go of a "character defect," especially when it's wired into your body as protection? In the next chapter, we'll explore the physical and emotional weight these traits carry and how surrendering them must also involve the body. Real letting go doesn't happen just in our heads; it happens when the body is finally ready to set something down.

11

STEP SEVEN: THE SOMATIC WEIGHT OF "CHARACTER DEFECTS"

"Humbly asked Him to remove our shortcomings."

THE SOMATIC WEIGHT OF SHORTCOMINGS

There's a quiet ache embedded in Step Seven—a moment where we stop striving, stop pretending, and humbly admit that we cannot change certain patterns on our own. At first glance, this Step sounds simple: identify what no longer serves us and ask for it to be removed. But when we look through a somatic lens, we see that what we call "shortcomings" are often much more than bad habits or character flaws, they are embodied survival patterns that once kept us safe.

The truth is, we didn't choose most of these responses consciously. Many of our reactive behaviors, such as shutting down, avoiding conflict, lashing out, controlling, isolating, and clinging, originated from places of emotional overwhelm. They were the nervous system's best attempt to protect us when we felt unsafe, unseen, or unloved. Our shortcomings are often not signs of failure but of pain left unprocessed and protection never unlearned.

Step Seven is not asking us to reject these parts of ourselves with shame but to release them with compassion and humility. But in order to let go, the body must first believe it's safe to do so. And for that, we must slow down and notice the weight we're carrying, not just emotionally but physiologically.

You may feel that weight on your shoulders when you try to hold everything together. In your jaw when you're bracing for criticism. In your gut, when you silence your needs to avoid rejection. These are not just emotional wounds; they are physical imprints of the roles we've played to survive.

As we begin to surrender these old patterns, the nervous system needs support. We don't release control, rage, or avoidance by force; we release them through safety, connection, and regulation. That's the deeper work of Step Seven: not begging for transformation but gently opening the body to receive it. It is humility, not humiliation, but an *honest reckoning with our limits* and a trust that something greater can meet us there.

And as those ingrained responses begin to shift, something profound happens: the body starts to trust that it no longer has to carry what it once did. Muscles soften. Breath deepens. Presence returns. What we referred to as shortcomings were often outdated strategies. And now, with help, spiritual and somatic, they can begin to fall away.

Step Seven offers this: not perfection, but permission to become who we are without the armor we once needed. One layer at a time.

THE SOMATIC SURRENDER

Step Seven asks us to become "entirely ready to have these defects of character removed." But in the somatic world, we don't speak in terms of defects; we speak in terms of *survival strategies*. What we're often trying to let go of in this step are not character flaws but protective adaptations: the tightened muscles, the defensive tone, and the emotional shutdowns that once kept us safe.

Letting go isn't an idea. It's a *physiological process.*

For someone in recovery, especially after long-term trauma or stress, the body doesn't release on command. It holds. It clings. It tightens around what's known, even if what's known is pain. That's not resistance. That's biology.

Malik's Unclenching

Malik had been sober just over a year when he came face to face with something that terrified him more than drinking again: his temper. He wasn't exploding like he used to, but the edge was still there. He found himself snapping at his partner over minor things, such as a tone, a delay, or a forgotten item. His voice would rise before he could stop it. His chest would tighten. And afterward, he'd sit in shame, hating the version of himself that showed up.

He thought Step Seven was about fixing this. About *removing* the defect. He wanted it gone. But in somatic therapy, something very different happened.

His therapist didn't ask, "Why are you so reactive?" Instead, she asked, "What happens in your body right before the heat rises?"

He paused. "My hands clench," he said quietly. "My jaw locks. My whole body braces, even though no one's attacking me." His therapist nodded and gently asked, "What would it be like to stay with that tension, without trying to fix it?"

They worked slowly. Week by week. Not dissecting his outbursts but learning to *feel* the buildup before the blow. He practiced pausing and feeling the buzz in his legs. Noticing the shift in his breath. Naming the signal before it became a storm.

One week later, Malik invited his partner to join the session. She sat beside him as he described what it felt like to brace for a fight even when there wasn't one. The therapist helped them explore what safety looked like in terms of tone, posture, and proximity. For the first time, Malik said out loud, "I'm not mad; I'm scared. I just didn't know how to say it."

That session changed everything.

They began practicing together. Before hard conversations, they'd take a few minutes to breathe, hand on chest. Sometimes, they'd go for a walk instead of sitting face to face. Malik didn't have to perform calmly anymore; he was learning how to *build* it in real time.

Over time, the rage softened. Not because it was erased, but because the body that once lived in constant alert was learning *I'm not in danger anymore*. Step Seven, for Malik, wasn't a purging of character defects. It was the moment he realized he didn't need to fight to feel safe. He needed to listen. To slow down. To trust the body that was finally learning how to let go.

The Body Doesn't Surrender by Force

In somatic healing, we know the nervous system does not let go just because we want it to. It lets go when it no longer *has* to protect. Readiness isn't a moral stance. It's a *felt sense* in the body that says, *I'm safe enough now to soften.*

Being "entirely ready" in Step Seven means that we have developed enough internal safety to begin *unclenching*. The shoulders drop. The breath deepens. The body begins to feel like a place we can inhabit, not manage. The parts of us that once jumped to fix, control, numb, or disappear begin to loosen under the weight of consistent, compassionate attention.

This isn't dramatic. It's subtle.

Letting go might feel like:

- Breathing through the urge to interrupt.
- Choosing stillness when chaos beckons.
- Feeling a tremble and not shutting it down.
- Saying, "I'm hurting," instead of lashing out.

This is somatic surrender. The moment the body stops gripping and starts allowing.

Repatterning the Body, Not Removing the Self

Step Seven is often misunderstood as a request for removal, a divine scrubbing away of our so-called defects. But through a somatic lens, Step Seven is not about erasing who we've been. It's about repatterning how we respond. The behaviors we once called "flaws"- controlling, numbing, withdrawing, lashing out were actually strategies. Protective reflexes that the body used to survive. They weren't moral failures. They were intelligent adaptations.

So when we ask to have these "defects" removed, what we're asking for is the capacity to respond differently. What was once automatic becomes intentional. What once felt like the only option becomes something we can set down with care. We don't punish the parts of ourselves that braced, tensed, or defended. We thank them. And then, with patience, we show them they're no longer needed.

Letting go in this context isn't an act of perfection; it's an act of presence. It's a quiet trust in the body's growing capacity to endure discomfort without collapsing or lashing out. It's the beginning of a new internal posture: one that moves from defense to openness.

Step Seven is a threshold. It's where we stop trying to force ourselves into better versions of who we think we should be and begin listening to what our body is already asking for: softness, breath, and relief. This is the sacred turning point where anger, shame, and control no longer need to be hidden or exiled. They can be acknowledged, integrated, and, over time, transformed.

We don't let go all at once. We let go as the body becomes ready. One breath. One muscle. One reflex at a time.

This is what it means to walk Step Seven somatically: to release not through effort but through safety. Not because we've conquered ourselves but because we've finally learned how to stay.

Chapter Summary

Step Seven is not about becoming perfect; it's about becoming willing. Willing to loosen our grip on the survival patterns that once protected us, even as they now keep us stuck. Through a somatic lens, this Step asks us not to cut away our flaws but to meet them with humility and compassion. These so-called "defects" are often the echoes of our pain, anger, control, avoidance, and learned strategies that once kept us safe.

True transformation doesn't happen by force. It occurs when the body begins to feel safe enough to relax and soften. Each time we pause instead of react, breathe instead of brace, stay instead of flee, we are repatterning ourselves from the inside out.

This is the quiet miracle of Step Seven: a shift from defense to presence, from self-judgment to self-trust. As we surrender what no longer serves us, we create space for peace, clarity, and connection.

And we prepare to turn outward from that space, softened, steadied, and hard-won. **Step Eight** calls us to acknowledge that our pain did not stay contained; it rippled outward, touching others in ways we may not have seen or were once too overwhelmed to face. Now, with a nervous system that no longer braces at every emotional turn, we begin the sacred work of relational accountability. Not just with apologies or explanations but with presence. With the inner capacity to stay grounded, to hear hard truths, to sit with discomfort, and to begin repairing what can be repaired. This next step isn't about rehearsed regret but embodied responsibility. *And it begins now.*

12

STEP EIGHT: THE BODY REMEMBERS, AND SO DO OTHERS

"Made a list of all persons we had harmed, and became willing to make amends to them all."

OTHERS REMEMBER, TOO

By the time we arrive at Step Eight, we've begun to unearth the roots of our own suffering. We've traced the internal patterns that shaped our choices, and we've asked for help in letting them go. But now, the healing must expand. Now, we are called to look outward, to turn our attention not just to what we've been through but to what others may still carry because of us.

Others remember, too, not just with their minds but their *bodies.*

Our actions, whether loud and explosive or quiet and avoidant, left impressions on the nervous systems of the people around us. Just as we learned to brace against abandonment, betrayal, or chaos, so did they. Just as our body adapted to survive, so did theirs. Our dysregulation, absences, and reactions didn't happen in a vacuum; they were felt, absorbed, and interpreted in real time.

Step Eight invites us to acknowledge this, not with shame, but with reverence. This is not about rehashing every misstep or begging for forgiveness. It is about becoming *willing* to name what was true. To see our impact without minimizing it. We must honor the ways others may still hold tension, mistrust, or grief when they remember us.

And just as our own healing has required safety and pacing, so too must our efforts toward amends be grounded in somatic readiness and nervous system care. This step is not about forcing repair. It's about preparing, gently, truthfully, and with deep integrity, to meet the echoes of our past with presence. Because others remember, and so must we. Not to punish ourselves but to make healing real.

PAIN DOESN'T LIVE IN A VACUUM, AND NEITHER DOES HEALING

Step Eight asks us to take inventory, not of things but of people. It shifts our focus from internal healing to relational responsibility. While earlier steps centered on how we were hurt, Step Eight invites us to widen the lens. It asks us to recognize that while our pain may have been personal, it was never private.

Our behavior, especially in active addiction or survival mode, had ripple effects. During those times, we often moved through the world disconnected from our bodies or overwhelmed by them. We were tense, reactive, shut down, or emotionally absent. Even if we didn't mean to cause harm, those around us felt the impact of our unpredictability, avoidance, irritability, or emotional withdrawal.

When the body is in distress and constantly bracing, avoiding, or numbing, it becomes difficult to stay present in relationships. Children may have felt unsure of our mood. Partners may have sensed our distance even if we were in the same room. Friends may have experienced us as inconsistent or unreachable. These patterns, whether loud and chaotic or quiet and avoidant, disrupted the emotional safety of those around us.

Step Eight is where we begin to take ownership of this, not from a place of shame but from a place of integrity. This is not about blaming ourselves for every painful moment. It's about recognizing how our pain may have shaped someone else's experience. It's about looking honestly at how our nervous systems, shaped by trauma and survival, affected the environments we were part of.

The clarity that arises here can be uncomfortable. We may remember faces, silences, missed moments, or words we wish we could take back. But this discomfort isn't meant to defeat us. It is meant to reconnect us, bringing us back into a relationship with the truth of what happened and with the people who were affected.

Healing, in this sense, becomes more than individual work. As we reconnect with our bodies, learning to slow down, soften, and stay present, we also become more attuned to others. We become less reactive, less withdrawn, and more able to engage with care. Step Eight is not just about preparing to make amends. It's about becoming someone whose presence causes less harm. Someone whose body no longer needs to push love away to feel safe.

This step invites us to see the past clearly, yes, but also to begin showing up differently in the present. Not by force but by choice. Not perfectly, but with awareness. It reminds us that the work we do to heal ourselves reaches far beyond us. And in that truth, something quiet but powerful begins to shift: **we begin to feel ready to repair.**

PREPARING THE BODY FOR RELATIONAL REPAIR: A SOMATIC APPROACH TO STEP EIGHT

Before we can make meaningful amends, we must prepare our internal landscape. It's not enough to create a list; we need to develop the somatic capacity to face that list name by name while staying grounded, present, and emotionally regulated. Step Eight isn't just an exercise in memory or moral clarity; it's a step that demands nervous system readiness. And this readiness must be built from the body up.

In somatic therapy, the body is seen as a source of emotional memory and unconscious reaction. Every person we place on our Step Eight list carries a relational charge: an imprint of past emotion, unresolved tension, or stored conflict. When we think of these individuals, our body often responds before our mind catches up. The heart may race. The breath may tighten. We might feel heat rise in the chest or tension in the jaw. These responses are not signs of failure or avoidance; they are somatic cues that signal unprocessed emotional material.

Somatic theory teaches us that these bodily reactions are not random; they are learned survival strategies encoded through past experiences. They reveal where the body still anticipates harm or rejection and where it might still be bracing against the discomfort of facing accountability. These reactions are messages, whether they look like defensiveness, avoidance, emotional numbness, or collapse. The goal is not to override them but to attune to them and build the capacity to stay with them without being overtaken.

This is why Step Eight is not about immediate action. It's about developing tolerance and regulation. In somatic terms, we need to work with *activation, noticing how charged we feel in the body,* and begin to build tools to stay with those sensations rather than acting from them. Practices such as grounding, breathwork, containment, and orienting help create the internal space to reflect honestly without becoming overwhelmed or shutting down.

For some names on the list, staying present may be easy. For others, simply imagining a conversation may cause the body to tense up or the mind to disconnect. That's not a barrier; it's information. Somatic healing reminds us that readiness is not a mindset; it's a state. And that state must be nurtured gently and consistently over time.

We prepare for external repair and build internal resilience by approaching Step Eight somatically. We learn to feel the discomfort of accountability without collapsing into shame or defensiveness. We develop the capacity to stay in truth, not just speak it. And that somatic steadiness becomes the foundation for all the relational repair that follows in Step Nine.

We don't confront the past all at once. We build somatic stamina in the present. Here's how:

Reclaim Your Inner Landscape

- Go outside. Walk slowly while naming aloud the safe things you see: trees, clouds, grass, birds. Let your eyes move gently, and name what's not threatening. This is orienting. It teaches your brain and body: "Right now, I am safe."

Soothing Touch with Intention

- Wrap your arms around your torso like a hug, or hold your own hand. Breathe into the contact. This gesture tells your nervous system: "You are not alone in this."

Micro-Imagery Practice

- Instead of visualizing the entire interaction, imagine just a second: a door opening, a hello, a shared breath. Then come back to the present and touch something grounding: your seat, your feet, a tree. Let the body know: "That's enough for now."

Pause the Loop

- When your mind spirals into fear, pause. Place one hand on your belly. One breath. One sound (hum, sigh, or exhale). One moment of stillness. Then, decide if you want to continue or gently step away.

These practices aren't about perfection. They're about preserving your capacity. You are allowed to go slowly. Repair begins with presence, not performance.

This is what makes Step Eight different. We're not forcing repair; we're embodying the possibility of it. That shift is radical. It changes not only how we relate to others but how we carry ourselves in the world.

HUMILITY AS RELATIONAL SURRENDER

By the time we reach Step Eight, we have already begun to cultivate humility internally. We've acknowledged our limitations, surrendered control, and allowed something greater to begin guiding our recovery. But now, we're being asked to bring that humility into a relationship, to allow it to *live in our nervous system* as we prepare to re-engage with the people we've impacted.

Humility in this step is not performative. It's not about apologizing excessively or playing the martyr. It's not about groveling. It's about remaining fully present in the discomfort of relational truth without needing to defend, explain, or rescue ourselves.

And that takes a deeply regulated body.

When we lack nervous system safety, relational humility is nearly impossible. Our body wants to protect itself. We may try to rationalize the harm we caused, minimize our role, or focus on our own pain to avoid accountability. These responses are understandable; they emerge when our system feels unsafe. But they also block the possibility of genuine repair.

True humility emerges when we can stay physically present in the face of relational tension. We keep our heart open, our breath steady, and our shoulders soft. We don't rush to defend, escape, or shut down. Instead, we stay. We listen. We allow the other person's experience to exist alongside our own without needing to fix it, control it, or make it about us.

This level of surrender is incredibly vulnerable. It requires us to step out of our well-worn protective strategies and simply be human, with all the discomfort, imperfection, and grace that entails. It allows us to say: *"Yes, I did that. And I am still worthy of love. I am still becoming."*

When our nervous system is anchored, we can tolerate another person's pain *without making it about us*. We can tolerate the grief that comes when a relationship cannot be restored. We can tolerate the complexity of emotions, both our own and theirs, without trying to control the outcome.

This kind of humility is not a sign of weakness. It is embodied strength. It is the fruit of nervous system healing. It allows us to show up with dignity, take responsibility, and stay connected, even when it's hard.

SLOW REPAIR AND SOMATIC GRACE

Step Eight does not ask us to make amends. That's Step Nine's work. Step Eight asks us to prepare, to become ready, somatically and spiritually, to step into the process of relational repair. And readiness, in this context, is not a finish line. It is a practice.

We must learn how to hold ourselves through relational discomfort, how to track our body's signals, and how to honor our pacing. We must build the capacity to tolerate grief, regret, and the unknown, all of which may surface as we prepare to reconnect with people we have hurt.

Some of these relationships will be available for repair. Others will not. Some will welcome us back. Others will never speak to us again. Step Eight is not a bargaining chip. It is a *commitment to honesty and repair*, regardless of whether that repair is received.

This requires grace. A kind of inner spaciousness that says: *"I did what I could, and I will keep showing up with integrity."* Grace allows us to name the harm we caused *without erasing our own humanity*. It allows us to hold space for the pain of others without giving in to shame or defensiveness. And grace is only possible when our nervous system feels safe enough to be flexible, present, and open.

Slow repair honors the reality that the body heals in layers. That accountability is not a single moment but a lifelong practice. That transformation happens not through grand gestures but through a thousand tiny choices to stay present when it would be easier to run.

This is the invitation of Step Eight: to begin becoming the kind of person who doesn't just want to feel better but who wants to *live differently*. Someone who not only heals their own wounds but also takes part in healing the relational space between themselves and others.

It's not about fixing the past. It's about becoming safe in the present, to ourselves, and to others. It's about embodying the grace we once begged for and now begin to extend.

This is what it means to be ready.

Chapter Summary

Step Eight isn't about making amends; it's about preparing to. It's about becoming willing to face the relational impact of our past with honesty, humility, and nervous system readiness. We begin to see that others remember, too, not just in their minds but in their bodies as well. And so, we don't rush. We don't push. We build capacity, one name at a time.

This step lays the foundation for something deeper. It invites us to look at who we've hurt and how we show up in relationships today. We begin the slow process of becoming someone who can face the truth *and stay present in it*.

Only when we have honored this preparation, emotionally, spiritually, and *somatically*, do we move into **Step Nine**.

And now, we are ready to return to others, not with fear or urgency, but with presence, care, and the willingness to repair what we can.

13

STEP NINE: REPAIR WITH PRESENCE

"Made direct amends to such people wherever possible, except when to do so would injure them or others."

THE BODY MUST BE READY TO RETURN

Before we can make meaningful amends, our body must be able to revisit the memory of a relationship or a moment of harm without tipping into panic, shame, or emotional shutdown. Readiness isn't just about having the right words; it's about whether your body can stay present when you speak them.

For many of us, even thinking about facing someone we've hurt brings a wave of physical response: a tight throat, clenched jaw, racing heart, or a sudden emotional fog that makes everything feel far away. These are not signs of resistance or failure. They are protective reflexes, your body's way of saying, "This still feels dangerous."

Step Nine isn't about forcing your way through that discomfort. It's about learning to notice what your body is telling you and working with it gently. The real question becomes: *Can I approach this person and stay grounded while doing so? Can I feel my feet on the floor, my breath in my chest, my voice in my throat, even if the conversation is hard?*

This Step is sacred. It invites us to return to places of relational pain, not to relive them, but to begin reweaving trust, dignity, and repair. And reweaving only occurs when our body has sufficient internal safety to remain present. We can't do this work while bracing or shutting down. We do it when we feel steady enough to remain open, even when things don't go as planned.

Readiness here isn't just emotional; it's somatic. It's knowing how to feel the edge of overwhelm and take one small step back toward the center. It's having tools that let you return to yourself in the moment: a hand on your heart, a deep breath into your belly, a quiet reminder that you are here and you are safe.

Simple Practice: Ground Before Repair

Before a conversation, sit or stand somewhere quiet. Feel the weight of your body supported by the earth. Take three slow breaths. On each exhale, imagine softening the areas where you're holding tension, such as your jaw, hands, and shoulders. Speak your intention quietly: *"I want to stay present. I want to stay kind. I don't have to rush."* Let that be enough for now.

REPAIR HAPPENS IN THE NERVOUS SYSTEM FIRST

When most people think of making amends, they picture a conversation, an apology, a moment of truth, a gesture of righting what went wrong. But from a somatic perspective, real repair begins long before a single word is spoken. It begins inside the body, in the quiet, internal shift from defensiveness to presence.

When we've hurt someone, especially in repeated or deep ways, the memory of that harm doesn't just live in the mind. It lingers in the body. The way we once spoke, the tension in our face, the energy we carried, these things may still echo in the other person's nervous system. To approach them with genuine intention, we must approach them differently. Not just with better words but with a different presence. A calmer body. A softened stance. A slower rhythm.

This isn't performance; it's repair through physiology. We begin by regulating ourselves, not to manipulate the outcome, but to create the possibility of safety. Our grounded presence, quiet breath, and steadiness offer a message without words: *I'm not who I was when I caused you pain.*

Consider the story of Dani, who had emotionally lashed out at her sister throughout her years of active drinking. After two years of sobriety and much inner work, Dani reached out to make amends. But before she did, she spent weeks simply imagining the conversation, sitting in stillness, and observing what came up in her body. She noticed a quickening in her chest whenever she pictured her sister's face. She practiced breathing into that space, loosening the urge to defend herself. By the time she sat down across from her sister, her shoulders were low, her voice was steady, and her presence was clear, not because she had rehearsed a speech but because she had prepared her body to stay.

Repair is not about convincing someone to forgive us. It's about offering something different than what we once brought to the relationship. A slower pace. A willingness to hear hard things. A nervous system that can tolerate discomfort without shutting down or striking back.

And if a face-to-face conversation isn't possible, the work can still begin. We sit with the memory. We track our sensations. We breathe through the grief or regret that arises. This internal preparation is part of the healing; it allows us to build capacity, whether or not the other person is ready to engage.

Making amends isn't just about making things right; it's about restoring relationships and repairing the damage. It's about arriving in a new way. A regulated body is often the most honest apology we can offer. Before the words ever leave our lips, the repair has already begun.

Repair begins *long before* the words. It begins in the body.

SOMATIC PRACTICE FOR STEP NINE: THE EMBODIED AMENDS

Making amends is not just what we say. It's how we show up: regulated, rooted, and real. This practice prepares your body to offer a true energetic repair, even before a conversation begins.

The Grounded Offering Ritual

Gather a Natural Object

- Go outside and find a small stone, leaf, or flower, something that symbolizes honesty, humility, and presence. Choose one for each person you're preparing to make amends to.

Create a Physical Space for Intention

- At home or outdoors, lay these objects in a small circle. This becomes your Amends Altar, a place where truth is witnessed by the earth, not just by people.

Regulate Before the Ritual

- Sit quietly near your altar. Place one hand over your heart, the other on your belly. Inhale deeply for 4 counts, and exhale slowly for 6. Do this 5 times, letting your body settle into the moment.

Speak to the Stone (or Leaf or Flower)

- One by one, pick up each object. Speak aloud the name of the person it represents. Say the words you wish to offer them, not rehearsed, just honest. Let your tone be soft and grounded. Imagine your breath reaching them, not just your words.

Say only what your body can stay connected to. If you feel yourself tightening or dissociating, pause. Breathe. Place the object down gently.

Close the Ritual

- When finished, touch each object again and say:
- *"I am showing up differently now."*
- *"I carry the willingness to repair, even if they cannot receive it yet."*

Then return each object to the earth with care, bury it, place it in water, or set it in a sacred place.

Why It Matters

This practice allows you to embody humility and readiness without rushing the conversation. It aligns your nervous system with the energy of truth before any words are spoken. Whether or not the other person is ready, your body becomes the apology.

Amends are not measured by forgiveness. They are measured by embodiment.

OWNING THE IMPACT WITHOUT NEEDING REDEMPTION

One of the most essential and challenging aspects of Step Nine is recognizing that we may offer our most sincere and heartfelt amends and still not be received. The nervous system wants resolution. It wants closure. However, the truth is that we are not owed reconciliation. Our task is to *acknowledge the impact of our past behavior without becoming attached to being redeemed.*

When we offer amends from a dysregulated place, we often over-identify with guilt or rush to "fix" things to alleviate our own discomfort. This creates a subtle power dynamic; we're no longer attending to the person we hurt but instead trying to be absolved by them. This is another survival pattern masquerading as humility. It's still about *us*.

Step Nine asks us to engage from a regulated, grounded self. To say: *"This is what I did. I see the impact. I am here to take responsibility, not to be forgiven, not to be welcomed back, but to tell the truth."*

This level of presence requires deep nervous system regulation. It means staying grounded and connected even when facing discomfort or rejection. It's the ability to sit with another person's pain without shutting down or slipping into defensiveness.

Owning impact somatically means holding space in the body for the ripple effects of our actions and staying connected with ourselves while we do so. It means allowing the other person to feel what they feel without needing to change or manage their response.

The healing here is internal. We make amends because it realigns us with *our values, our sobriety, and our nervous system integrity*. We become the kind of person who can be trusted with the truth, even when that truth is hard to hear.

When we are no longer trying to be redeemed, we become *trustworthy*. And sometimes, that trust is the first real amends we ever make.

LIVING AMENDS, SACRED REPAIR

Step Nine may open with a direct conversation but continues in every interaction thereafter. Living amends are not just symbolic gestures; they are embodied practices of relational accountability that unfold over time. They are the daily, quiet proof that we are becoming someone new.

In many cases, especially when the person we harmed is unreachable, or reconciliation is unsafe, living amends are the *only* option. But they are no less sacred. In fact, they may be the truest reflection of our transformation.

Living amends happen when:

- We respond with presence instead of defensiveness.
- We tell the truth, even when it's uncomfortable.
- We honor boundaries, even when we want closeness.
- We show up consistently without demanding acknowledgment.
- We no longer spread our dysregulation into others' nervous systems.

Sometimes, we won't get the chance to speak our amends out loud. The door may be closed. The relationship may be too fragile. Or the person may no longer be in our lives. In those moments, the path to repair doesn't end; it simply shifts. It moves inward, into the body, into the life we live from this moment forward.

True amends, from a somatic perspective, are not just about apologies. They are about consistency. Repetition. Integrity in action. They are about the nervous system learning to respond differently and, through that, becoming someone new.

Take Marisol, for example. In her addiction, she would disappear for days, leaving her teenage son to wonder where she was and if she'd ever come back. Now three years sober, she's tried reaching out, but her son doesn't respond. She hasn't seen him in over a year.

Instead of chasing, Marisol began to focus on how she showed up in her everyday life. She started waking up at the same time each morning, eating nourishing meals, and treating those around her with the steady presence she wished she could offer her son. She kept a photo of him by her bed, not to ache with guilt, but as a quiet promise to live differently. When grief came, she didn't run. She sat with it. She breathed through the ache. Over time, her body stopped bracing and started opening. And that, too, became part of the amends.

Our nervous systems and the nervous systems of those we've hurt don't heal through words alone. They heal through the repetition of safety. Through grounded presence. Through quiet mornings where, we choose regulation over chaos. Through steady breathing instead of sharp reactions. We become the apology, not through what we say, but through how we live.

Living amends means walking through the world with a body that no longer harms. A body that no longer disappears. A body that listens, stays, and breathes, even when it's hard. It means understanding that trust won't come all at once. That relationship may not heal the way we hope. That some people may never feel safe with us again. And still, we keep showing up. For them. For ourselves.

In this light, Step Nine is less about closure and more about embodiment. It invites us to move through life with an unarmored nervous system that carries no demand, only presence. One that offers safety without insisting on a response.

This is a sacred repair. To let our nervous system say what our words cannot: *I'm here now. I'm steady. I will not abandon you again, not even in silence.*

Chapter Summary

Step Nine asked more of us than words; it asked for presence. To approach those we've harmed not from fear or performance but from a place of nervous system integrity. To show up in our bodies, steady and softened, with no demand for outcome, only the willingness to be accountable.

Whether our amends were accepted, rejected, or left unfinished, what mattered most was how we came to the moment: grounded, honest, and able to stay. That is the true amends. A body that no longer vanishes. A presence that no longer wounds. A life that moves with intention, not reactivity.

This step reminded us that healing isn't about fixing the past; it's about refusing to repeat it. Through embodied consistency, we become someone different. The past lives in us, but it no longer leads us. Our gestures grow quieter. Our nervous system is less armored. And in that space, we begin to relate, not just repair.

Step Nine marked the close of a chapter centered on recognition, release, and relational repair. But the work doesn't end here. What comes next are the living steps, **Ten, Eleven, and Twelve**. These are the practices that keep us present. That deepens our integration. That allows our recovery not only to sustain but also to serve.

This is where recovery becomes embodied. Ongoing. Alive.

Let's continue.

14

LIVING THE STEPS THROUGH THE BODY: STEPS TEN, ELEVEN, AND TWELVE

"A Daily Practice of Integration, Attunement, and Embodied Service"

STEP TEN: EMBODIED SELF-REFLECTION

"Continued to take personal inventory and when we were wrong promptly admitted it."

Step Ten is often framed as maintenance, but that word doesn't capture the quiet power of what's really happening here. This step marks the moment our recovery stops being reactive and becomes relational: with ourselves, others, and the sensations that arise within us daily.

For the somatic self, Step Ten is a daily return. A return to the body. A return to honesty. A return to alignment.

It's where we stop waiting for the chaos to wake us up and begin noticing the subtler signals: the clenched jaw before a lie, the tight chest before defensiveness, the holding of the breath when shame creeps in. These moments are our inventory. Not a moral checklist, but a felt sense of when we've shifted out of presence and into protection.

Lena's Story: Inventory from the Inside Out

Lena had been sober for nearly two years. Her life, on paper, was stable, with no slips, no crises, no dramatic fallouts. But inside, she was beginning to feel disconnected again. She caught herself snapping at coworkers, pulling away from her sponsor, forgetting meals, and losing sleep. The old tension in her stomach was back, and with it, the quiet thought: *Something's wrong, and I don't know what.*

When she sat down to do her nightly Step Ten, the old habit returned: write what she did *"wrong,"* circle what she needed to make amends for and move on. But the list felt shallow. So she tried something new. She placed one hand on her chest, the other on her belly, and just breathed.

It took a few minutes, but eventually, the truth surfaced, not in her mind, but in her body.

"I was holding my breath all day."

As she stayed with that awareness, her shoulders began to tremble. She realized she'd spent the last week in a state of bracing, defending, rushing, and avoiding quiet. The tension wasn't about a single wrong action. It was about not listening to herself. About overriding her need to rest, to feel, to soften.

That night, Lena's inventory didn't focus on what she had "done" but on what her body had been trying to say. And the next day, instead of apologizing out of guilt, she made small, embodied choices: she ate slowly, made eye contact, and called her sponsor not to perform but to connect. These weren't grand gestures, but they were different. They were real. They were regulated.

What Step Ten Looks Like Somatically

This step is no longer just a correction; it's a regulation tool. It helps us stay attuned to what's happening inside so we can adjust before the wreckage builds.

Here's how it works in practice:

- **Pause** before reacting. Notice if your breath is shallow, your shoulders are tight, and your jaw is locked. Ask: *What part of me is speaking right now, my protector or my presence?*
- **Track the sensations.** Instead of jumping to conclusions, name the feeling state: "My stomach is in knots," or "I feel heat rising in my face." That's inventory.
- **Ask your body what it needs.** Maybe it's a breath, a walk, a hand on your heart. Maybe it's the courage to speak a truth or the humility to say, "I need a moment."
- **Course-correct gently.** Step Ten isn't about shame. It's about honesty. We notice. We adjust. We return to connection.

In somatic language, we are developing ***interoception***, the ability to feel and interpret the signals inside us. We are learning to live inside our bodies with awareness, which means we can catch dysregulation early and respond with care.

This is what it means to *"promptly admit when we are wrong."* Not because we've broken a rule but because we've left ourselves. And through presence, we return.

STEP TEN AS A PRACTICE OF PRESENCE

This is where sobriety matures.

We are no longer holding on for dear life; we are learning to hold ourselves. We are not just trying to avoid relapse but building a life where peace becomes familiar, and chaos becomes the exception.

Through daily somatic inventory, we tend to the nervous system with care. We scan not only for external wreckage but for internal tension. We don't just look at what we did; we look at how we were. Were we regulated? Connected? Grounded? Did we breathe?

This step becomes our ongoing amends, not to others, but to the body we once abandoned. It's how we say, *I see you now. I will not ignore your signals. I will not leave you behind.*

And with each day of practice, we build a more honest life. One rooted in breath, in sensation, in choice. A life where integrity is not an idea; it's how we move, speak, and live.

Next, in Step Eleven, we deepen this presence. We move from noticing to listening, from reacting to receiving. Not just from ourselves but from something greater. In that space, the body becomes not only our compass but our altar.

Step Eleven: Listening for Guidance Through the Body

"Sought through prayer and meditation to improve our conscious contact with God as we understood Him..."

By Step Eleven, we've cleared space: space in our lives, in our relationships, and most importantly, in our bodies. We've softened the bracing, released some of the shame, and learned how to stay present in the face of discomfort. Now, that space becomes sacred. This is the step where we stop *talking* to our Higher Power and start *listening*.

For many in recovery, prayer and meditation can feel loaded. Maybe we carry wounds from religion, confusion about God, or discomfort with the very idea of faith. But in somatic recovery, spirituality doesn't have to begin with belief. It can begin with *sensation*.

Because spiritual connection isn't just an idea; it's an experience. And the body is where that experience takes root.

Jim's Story: The First Time He Felt God

Jim had been sober for over a year when he reached Step Eleven. He still bristled at the word "God," and his sponsor knew it. "Forget the language," his sponsor told him. "Just sit. Be still. Try listening, instead of asking."

So Jim did. One morning, sitting at the edge of his bed, he placed both feet on the floor and took a breath. Then another. No special posture. No prayer. Just a quiet moment before the noise of the day started.

He noticed how tight his chest was, how his hands had curled into fists. He didn't try to fix it. He just noticed.

And after a few minutes, something changed.

It wasn't dramatic. His shoulders dropped a little. His breath came easier. A single tear slid down his cheek, not because he was sad, but because, for the first time in a long while, he didn't feel alone.

He didn't hear a voice. He didn't have a vision. But something inside him shifted. A small, quiet knowing: *I'm okay. I'm here. I'm held.*

That was the moment Jim began to understand that prayer didn't have to be spoken, and God didn't have to be named. He'd found connection, not in a church or in a book, but in his breath. In his body. In presence.

What Step Eleven Looks Like Somatically

Step Eleven teaches us that spiritual connection doesn't live in our thoughts. It lives in the body. The soft moments. The regulated nervous system. The breath that deepens without being forced.

We might recognize this guidance as:

- A calm in the center of the chest.
- A spontaneous sigh of relief.
- A sense of clarity that feels more like remembering than figuring out.
- An ease in our movements, like our body is no longer fighting itself.

Instead of praying for answers, we sit with *presence*. Instead of meditating to get somewhere, we meditate to *arrive*. Somatic spirituality is less about speaking and more about sensing.

We begin to ask:

- What does peace feel like in my body?
- Where do I notice openness or softening when I feel aligned?
- How does fear feel different from intuition?
- Can I pause long enough to *feel* when I'm being guided?

Step Eleven is not about control; it's about communion.

Step Eleven as a Practice of Embodied Trust

This step is where prayer becomes listening, and meditation becomes noticing. We are not trying to *figure life out* anymore. We're learning to *follow what feels true*: in our breath, in our gut, in the silent pull of the body toward or away from certain people, actions, and choices.

And when guidance doesn't come easily, we don't force it. We return to the body. We place a hand on the heart. We soften the shoulders. We say *I'm here. I'm listening.*

That act alone is a prayer.

And what we begin to discover is this: we were never disconnected. We were just too braced to hear.

Step Eleven isn't about perfection. It's about *practice*. And each time we choose stillness over striving, sensing over forcing, presence over panic, we open ourselves to something greater. Not above us, but *within us*.

In Step Twelve, we carry this integration into the world. We become the safe place, the listening presence, the quiet invitation. Service becomes not just an act but an embodiment. And that's where real transformation begins.

Step Twelve – Embodied Service and Nervous System Stewardship

"Having had a spiritual awakening as the result of these steps, we tried to carry this message to alcoholics, and to practice these principles in all our affairs."

Step Twelve is not the final step. It's the first step again. But this time, we're walking with different feet, in a different body, with a nervous system that's been rewired by honesty, safety, connection, and truth. We've surrendered. We've repaired. We've listened. And now, we're ready to give back.

But this service isn't just what we do. It's *how we show up*.

We become a safe place in a world full of threat signals. We become someone whose presence no longer dysregulates a room. Someone whose stillness helps others breathe deeper. Someone who knows how to pause, how to soften, how to stay.

This is what it means to carry the message, not just in words but in **the integrity of the nervous system.**

Jim's Story: Becoming the Message

Jim didn't think he'd ever sponsor anyone. "I'm too messed up," he told his sponsor. "I'm still figuring this out."

But one night, at a meeting, a newcomer named Luis sat beside him, twitching, scanning the room, barely able to stay in his seat. Jim remembered that feeling, the buzz of panic beneath the skin, the overwhelming shame, the body still detoxing from years of pain.

After the meeting, Jim didn't try to say anything wise. He didn't offer advice. He just turned toward Luis, softened his voice, and said, "Hey. I've been there."

Luis nodded, eyes welling. That's all it took. No script. No solution. Just presence.

They started meeting weekly. Jim didn't teach Luis how to be perfect; he helped him learn how to stay. To breathe. To feel safe in his own skin for maybe the first time ever.

And through those slow, patient conversations, Jim realized something: *he had become the message*. Not because he had all the answers. But because he knew how to sit with someone without flinching.

Because he had stayed long enough to feel his own healing, and now he could help someone else find theirs.

Embodied Service: What Step Twelve Looks Like in the Body

Service is often seen as action, bringing a meeting into detox, showing up early to make coffee, and sponsoring someone new. And those things *matter deeply*. But at its core, Step Twelve asks: ***Who are you becoming?*** What kind of nervous system do you bring into the room?

Trauma has a way of spreading, much like a contagion. However, the concept of safety can similarly be transmitted, offering a beacon of hope.

When we serve from a regulated place, we model recovery in the body, not just in behavior. Our calm tone, ability to pause, and capacity to stay when someone cries, rages, or dissociates are living amends to the world.

We become:

- A **co-regulator** for someone still living in a state of survival.
- A **witness** to stories others have never shared out loud.
- A **guide** not through perfection but through presence.

Carrying the Message Somatically

To practice Step Twelve somatically, we begin each day with awareness:

- *Where am I in my body?*
- *Am I grounded enough to help, or do I need to pause and anchor first?*
- *Can I be a safe place, or do I need to come back to my own before I reach out to others?*

We serve best not when we forget ourselves but when we stay connected to ourselves while holding space for others.

Step Twelve becomes the art of returning, again and again, to the basics:

- Breathe.
- Listen.
- Stay.
- Don't fix.
- Don't flee.
- Just be there, fully.

Step Twelve: Integration, Service, and the Sacred Circle of Sobriety

Step Twelve is not a destination. It's a sacred return. We do not arrive here with the illusion that we're done. We arrive with humility, ready to begin again.

We return to Step One's surrender not because we've slipped but because we now know that healing doesn't follow a straight line. It moves in circles, a rhythm of remembering, forgetting, and remembering again. We revisit the honesty of Step Four not to shame ourselves but because truth has become an act of compassion. And we practice the self-awareness of Step Ten not to punish or perfect ourselves but because staying grounded in the present means more to us now than proving we've *"got it all together."*

Each act of service doesn't deplete us; it roots us more deeply into our own recovery. Every time we sit with another alcoholic in their fear, confusion, or grief, we aren't just offering them a sense of safety; we're reminding our own nervous system that we're still safe, too. We're still sober. We're still here. Step Twelve isn't about being the perfect sponsor or saying all the right things; it's about becoming a steady, regulated presence that communicates hope before we even open our mouths. Our body tells the truth before our voice does. And the truth it speaks is simple, powerful, and unforgettable: *You are not alone. You are not broken. And there is a way through.*

Your calm becomes a form of medicine. Your groundedness becomes a lifeline. Your honesty becomes a quiet invitation to trust. This is the miracle of embodiment, not fixing or preaching, but becoming the message itself. Through our presence, we offer something words alone cannot carry: the nervous system's living proof that healing is possible. That recovery is real.

Just when we think we've given all we have, we find that true service doesn't drain us; it fills us. It leads us back to humility, to gratitude, to the core of Step One, where we first admitted we couldn't do this alone. Step Twelve is not the end of the journey but the widening of it. It's not about completion; it's about continuity. This is the long arc of recovery: not perfection, but participation. Not fixing ourselves or others, but showing up over and over again as someone willing to stay, to feel, to soften, and to serve.

The first nine steps cracked us open and helped us begin to repair what we had lost. The last three have rooted us in daily practice and deep presence. This is the moment when recovery stops being something we *do* and becomes who we *are*. We are no longer running. We are no longer hiding. We are no longer bracing for the next crash. We are here. We are home. We are ready.

And somewhere out there, someone is still lost in the dark, scared, raw, on the edge of letting go. May your presence be what reminds them of the truth we've all had to learn: *we heal, we stay, we rise - together.*

Chapter Summary: Steps 10, 11, and 12 – Returning Through the Body

Steps Ten, Eleven, and Twelve form the sacred rhythm of sustained recovery. They are not a conclusion but a continuous spiral, an invitation to revisit, re-ground, and re-embody the truths we've uncovered along the way.

Step Ten teaches us to stay awake, to notice when old patterns return, and not to judge but to restore integrity gently and swiftly. In somatic terms, it's the daily practice of checking in with the body: Where am I holding? What am I avoiding? What needs to be named?

It's self-inquiry, not self-attack. A return to truth through the sensations that speak louder than words.

Step Eleven opens us to deeper contact, not only with a Higher Power but with our own inner stillness. We begin to trust the wisdom of silence, of breath, of the spaces between thoughts. Prayer may take the shape of movement. Meditation might look like sitting in the sunlight with our hand on our heart. In these moments, we're not performing belief; we're embodying connection. The divine begins to live in the quiet places of our body, where panic once sat.

Step Twelve brings it full circle, showing us that recovery is not merely for us; it's through us. As we serve others, we become vessels of regulation, steadiness, and hope. Our presence carries a message even when our mouths don't. We walk into dark places with others not to rescue but to remind us that healing is possible because we are living proof.

These three steps ask us not to graduate but to integrate. We begin again and again, not because we're broken, but because we've discovered a sacred way of living: honest, embodied, connected. What once felt like the end now reveals itself as a deeper beginning.

As we move into Chapter Fifteen, we explore the foundation beneath these final steps: *embodied spirituality*. What does it mean to feel God, not just think about God? What does the soul sound like in the nervous system's language? How does the body become a sanctuary rather than a battleground?

This next chapter invites us to discover a spirituality that doesn't require belief, only presence. One that lives in the lungs, the belly, and the bones. A spirituality that stays when everything else has fallen away.

15

BEYOND THE STEPS – A SOMATIC PATH FOR EVERY RECOVERY JOURNEY

Recovery isn't one-size-fits-all. It never was. You don't have to work the 12 Steps to be part of the recovery conversation. You don't have to call yourself an alcoholic, go to daily meetings, or recite prayers to reclaim your body, your voice, or your future. While this book has focused on integrating somatic principles into the traditional 12-Step framework, the truth is that these body-based practices are not exclusive to any program. They are human practices. They belong to anyone who is healing.

Today, there are many paths to sobriety and wholeness. Some people walk through the rooms of AA or NA and find safety there. Others choose Refuge Recovery, Recovery Dharma, She Recovers, The Phoenix, SMART Recovery, or Women for Sobriety. Some find healing in trauma therapy, spiritual communities, yoga studios, or wilderness retreats. Still, others recover in silence, without a program, drawing on their own wisdom, resilience, and desire for something different.

This chapter is for those who took a different path. It's for the people who walked into a meeting and never went back—not because they didn't want help, but because it didn't speak their language. It's for those who didn't hit a dramatic "rock bottom," but quietly realized their life needed to change. It's for the ones who are still using, still struggling, still surviving, not because they're broken, but because their nervous system hasn't yet found a safe place to land.

If that's you, I want you to know that you're not missing anything. You haven't failed. You haven't fallen behind. You've simply taken a different path, and this somatic work can walk with you.

The truth is that recovery, no matter the path, requires more than willpower. It requires safety. It requires learning to live in your body again without fear. Trauma is stored in the tissues. Disconnection lives in the breath. And healing begins when we start listening to the signals we've spent years trying to outrun.

Somatic practices don't require belief or doctrine. They only ask you to begin where you are. With sensation. With breath. With a willingness to turn toward your experience instead of away from it. This chapter isn't here to tell you how to recover. It's here to remind you that wherever you are, your body still wants you back. You belong in this work. You belong in your healing.

WHY THE BODY BELONGS IN EVERY RECOVERY STORY

No matter how you define recovery or whether you even use that word, the truth is this: the body always remembers. It remembers the panic before the drink, the numbness after the binge, the tightening in your chest every time you promised, *"This is the last time."* It remembers what it was like to survive.

Addiction, at its core, is often a survival response. It's not just a set of poor decisions or weak willpower. It's a way the nervous system adapts when it doesn't feel safe when pain, trauma, or loneliness become too much to carry without some form of escape. That's why no matter what program or path you follow, *healing has to include the body.* You can change your thoughts, rewrite your story, or even quit a substance. However, if your nervous system still feels under threat, it will keep pulling you back into the same protective patterns.

Somatic recovery isn't about achieving peace all at once; it's about slowly rebuilding safety inside your skin. It's about noticing the subtle language of sensation and beginning to respond with compassion rather than urgency. It's a conversation between the body and the present moment that gently rewires our ability to stay.

This isn't theoretical. It's deeply practical. When someone in recovery begins to notice that they clench their jaw every time they feel criticized, that's somatic awareness. When they place their hand on their chest before making a hard decision and wait for the breath to return, that's somatic regulation. When they recognize that their spiral into shame is accompanied by a drop in body temperature or a sudden urge to lie down, that's the body offering information, not punishment, but a signal.

And the beauty of somatic work is that it meets you exactly where you are. You don't need to be sober for a certain number of days, have a sponsor, or attend a certain number of meetings. You just need a body. A body that is willing to begin the slow, sacred work of feeling again.

Practice: Come Back to Now

Wherever you are, pause. Feel the weight of your body on the chair, the floor, or your feet.

- Let your eyes gently scan the space around you.
- Find one thing that feels grounding: its color, texture, or weight.
- Let your breath find its way back. No forcing. Just noticing.
- Whisper to yourself: *"This moment is safe enough to stay."*

In this chapter, we'll explore how somatic recovery tools can be used by anyone, regardless of their spiritual beliefs, recovery affiliation, or history. Whether you're working the Steps, exploring mindfulness, or simply trying to feel less chaotic, your body holds the key to coming home.

WHAT SOMATIC RECOVERY CAN LOOK LIKE (NO STEPS REQUIRED)

Somatic recovery doesn't require a workbook, a sponsor, or a perfect morning routine. It begins in the body, in small, consistent choices to turn toward your experience instead of away from it. These choices don't have to follow a program. They just need to follow your body's rhythm, moment to moment.

Whether you're newly sober, exploring harm reduction, or years into a recovery journey without labels or rules, these core somatic principles apply. Each one offers a way to build safety inside yourself, not through force, but through presence.

- *Start Where You Are: Safety Before Insight*

You don't need to understand your trauma to begin healing. You don't have to figure out why you're triggered before you respond. Your nervous system doesn't need explanations; it needs support.

Start by asking simple questions: *What am I feeling right now, in my body? Where is it, tight, hot, heavy, or tense?* Notice without needing to fix.

Practice: Ground Through the Senses

When your thoughts spiral or your body feels flooded, this simple sensory practice can help bring you back to the present. It gently shifts your attention away from internal overwhelm and reconnects you to the environment around you. You are reminding your nervous system: *We are here. We are now. We are safe enough.*

Try this:

Look around and name out loud or silently:

- **5 things you can see** – Notice colors, shapes, light, or movement.

- **4 things you can touch** – Run your hands over your clothing, the chair beneath you, or the texture of a nearby object.
- **3 things you can hear** – Tune in to background noise: birds, a hum of the fridge, traffic outside, your breath.
- **2 things you can smell** – Breathe in and notice subtle scents. If nothing stands out, scratch an orange peel, open a lotion bottle, or imagine a smell you love.
- **1 thing you can taste or imagine tasting** – Sip water, chew gum, or simply bring to mind the taste of mint, chocolate, or something comforting.

Why it works:

This method activates the orienting reflex in your nervous system—a primal survival function that helps you assess your surroundings. Instead of staying stuck in trauma loops, fight/flight/freeze responses, or emotional overwhelm, you're anchoring yourself in the here and now. The body begins to shift from threat response toward regulation.

Tips for deepening the practice:

- Pair it with slow, conscious breathing.
- Pause for a few seconds between each sense.
- If a particular sense feels inaccessible (for example, taste or smell), skip it or imagine instead.
- Use it as a daily check-in, not just in crisis. It builds your baseline capacity to stay present.

Remember:

Grounding isn't about forcing calm. It's about returning. You're not trying to fix your feelings—you're letting your body know it's allowed to feel them, safely, in this moment.

❖ *Movement Is Medicine*

Sometimes, stillness feels anything but safe. For people healing from trauma or addiction, sitting still can stir up discomfort, flashbacks, or restlessness. That doesn't mean you're doing something wrong—it means your body may need to *move* in order to settle. Somatic recovery honors this. Movement becomes medicine, not as a workout, but as a gentle signal that helps the nervous system shift out of freeze or hyperarousal.

Try this simple regulation ritual:

1. **Stand (or sit) somewhere you feel relatively safe.**
2. If standing, plant your feet firmly. If seated, feel the support beneath you.
3. **Begin at your hands.**
4. Gently shake your wrists—loose, relaxed, no pressure. Then let the motion ripple into your forearms, shoulders, chest, and hips. Let it travel down through your legs and ankles.
5. **Let the movement be organic.**
6. You might bounce slightly on your heels. You might sway side to side. You might release a sigh or a sound as you exhale. There's no "right" way—just what feels like *something is moving.*
7. **Stay with it for 30 seconds to a minute.**
8. Then pause. Notice any shift in sensation—heat, tingling, release, breath. Repeat if needed.

Why it works:

Shaking is one of the body's oldest self-regulation tools. In animals, it's how the body discharges survival energy after a threat. In humans, it helps move stuck fight/flight energy and reconnects us to presence after overwhelm. You're not performing, you're discharging, resetting, reclaiming your space inside your skin.

When to use it:

- After a difficult conversation
- When you feel frozen or numb
- Before or after sharing something vulnerable
- Anytime your body feels full of "too much" or "not enough"

Reminder:

You're not trying to "calm down"—you're letting your body *come back online*. Movement doesn't mean you're avoiding your feelings. It means you're supporting them, giving them somewhere to go.

- ***Let Breath Be the Anchor, Not the Solution***

Breath is powerful, but for many trauma survivors, deep breathing can feel unsafe or too intense at first. Start gently. Don't try to control the breath. *Just notice it.* Let it become your companion rather than your controller.

Practice: Track the Breath

- Place one hand on your chest and one on your belly.
- Feel the natural rise and fall—no need to deepen. Just feel.
- Whisper to yourself: *"I don't have to change this. I have to notice."*
- This builds tolerance for being with sensation safely.

❖ *Find Your Regulating Tools (That Actually Work for You)*

Not every tool works for everybody. Somatic recovery is personal. It's a practice of trying, noticing, adjusting, and trying again. Your regulating tools may not be what others use, and that's okay.

Some people feel grounded when they press their feet into the floor. Others calm when they smell essential oils or squeeze a stress ball. Some slow down by washing their hands in warm water. These aren't tricks; they're *signals* to your nervous system that it's safe to soften.

Practice: Build a Somatic Safety List

Write down 5 things (touch, sound, movement, visual, breath) that help you feel "a little better."

Use this list when you feel off. Don't wait for a crisis. These are your body's doorways back to presence.

❖ *Connection Regulates*

Even if you don't feel ready for therapy or community, safe human contact is one of the most powerful somatic tools. Our nervous systems are wired for co-regulation, which means we are calm in the presence of someone who is regulated, kind, and steady.

The connection doesn't have to be deep or long. It can be a brief phone call, a text, or a smile exchanged. It can also be internal, placing your hand on your heart and whispering to yourself like you would a scared child. You can be your own first safe person.

Practice: Mini Co-Regulation

When you feel overwhelmed or disconnected, try reaching out to someone whose presence helps calm your system. If no one is available, play a recording of a soothing voice—something familiar, steady, and kind. Let yourself settle as you listen. Sit quietly. Let your body respond.

You might say aloud, or hear someone say: *"You're not alone. You're safe enough to feel this."*

This is the heart of somatic recovery. It's not about mastering a technique—it's about practicing presence, moment by moment, pattern by pattern. You begin again not because you've figured everything out, but because you remember that today, you can stay with yourself.

These tools aren't just for those following a traditional recovery path. They're for anyone reclaiming their inner safety. Because real recovery isn't about conforming to someone else's system—it's about learning how to come home to your own.

Somatic Relapse Repair – Reclaiming Safety After Slipping

Relapse doesn't only happen to those in 12-Step programs. It can happen to anyone who has made the brave decision to face their addiction, whether through therapy, spiritual work, medication-assisted treatment, or simply one day at a time on their own terms. This section is for you, too.

No matter how you got sober or how you're staying sober, relapse can feel devastating. But it is not proof that you've failed. It is not a moral flaw. It is not the undoing of all your work. It is information. It is your body's way of saying *something became too much.*

For many of us, relapse has been framed as weakness, self-sabotage, or a lack of commitment. But what if we looked at it somatically? What if relapse was a nervous system response, a desperate attempt to return to regulation when all other resources were out of reach?

The body doesn't reach for alcohol, drugs, food, or compulsions because it doesn't care about our healing. It reaches because it's overwhelmed. Because the pain, the numbness, the disconnection felt unbearable. And in that moment, the body remembered what used to soothe, even if it came with a cost.

When we understand relapse through this lens, everything shifts. We move from shame to inquiry. From punishment to repair.

Somatic relapse repair begins not with guilt but with gentleness. It asks:

- *Where did I lose my sense of safety?*
- *What sensations did I ignore?*
- *What was I running from—or reaching for?*

These aren't questions to scold ourselves. They're questions to understand ourselves, to reclaim a relationship with the body that is rooted in compassion, not control.

Often, relapse follows early somatic signs, such as shallow breathing, racing thoughts, clenched muscles, sudden exhaustion, or a deep sense of emptiness. These aren't just symptoms. They're signals. They're the body whispering, "I'm in danger," even when no danger is visible.

We were not taught to listen to these signs. We were taught to override them, to pretend we were fine, to push through. But that pushing creates fractures. Somatic relapse repair means pausing to mend them, not by starting over, but by starting again from where we are.

In this framework, relapse is not the end. It's a rupture. And repair happens through *presence*, *regulation*, and *relationship*, not force. We begin again not because we failed but because we're still here. Still worthy. Still willing to heal.

You don't need a chip, a group, or a specific label to reclaim yourself. You just need honesty. And your body.

You are not broken. You are responding to something overwhelming. And that response deserves **tenderness**, not judgment.

Jason's Story: After the Shatter

Jason had been sober for over five years. He wasn't part of a 12-Step program. Still, he worked closely with a therapist, stayed connected to his recovery circle, and practiced daily meditation and journaling. His recovery was solid. It felt like a part of him, earned, lived, and embodied.

Then, one morning, everything fell apart.

His younger brother, his best friend, died suddenly in a car accident. No warning. No time to brace. Just a knock on the door and a life torn away.

Jason tried to hold steady. He leaned on his tools. He checked in with his therapist. But grief lives in the body. And Jason's nervous system was no longer online. His breath became tight. His hands trembled.

He couldn't sleep or eat. He couldn't cry. Numbness wrapped around him like armor. And one night, he relapsed.

The shame was instant. But so was the insight. This time, he didn't spiral. He didn't isolate. He called a friend and said, *"I broke. I don't know what else to do."*

The next day, Jason sat with his somatic therapist. Not to explain himself but to feel. He didn't start by talking. He started with breath. With movement. With shaking. With silence. He curled into himself and sobbed. His body had held the trauma too tightly, for too long.

That moment didn't erase his relapse. But it reframed it. It became the beginning of his return.

Jason is sober again now, not because he was perfect, but because he chose presence over performance. He says, *"Relapse didn't undo my recovery. It showed me where the next layer of healing had to begin."*

STAYING REGULATED – PREVENTING RELAPSE THROUGH SOMATIC INTEGRATION

Relapse prevention isn't about gripping harder. It's about softening sooner.

When we think of staying sober, most of us imagine it as a battle: white-knuckling, resisting, doing whatever it takes to avoid "going back." But what if it wasn't about resistance at all? What if the real strength lies in noticing the early signs *and responding with care before the collapse?*

Relapse doesn't begin with a drink or a drug. It begins with a shift inside the body. A tightening of the jaw. A shallowing of breath. A sudden urge to isolate. The nervous system starts to tip out of regulation, and before we even realize it, we're bracing again. Numb again. Alone again.

Somatic integration teaches us to listen to these early whispers instead of waiting for a scream. It's not about being perfect. It's about *being present* enough to notice when we've left ourselves and gentle enough to return.

This kind of awareness is built through rhythm, not rules. A few minutes of breath before a hard conversation. A walk after a triggering memory. A hand on the heart before opening your phone. These moments aren't dramatic, but they're decisive. They're how we stay.

When you practice somatic integration, you're not trying to "beat addiction." You're learning how to *tend to the body before it has to reach for something to cope.* You're building a nervous system that can handle more life, more joy, more grief, more quiet, and more intimacy without shutting down or burning out.

You're not just surviving. You're strengthening your capacity to feel and stay safe at the same time.

Recovery is not a finish line; it's a *felt sense* of stability. It's not a checklist; it's a *relationship* with your body that grows in trust each time you choose to pause, to listen, to stay.

You will still have hard days. You may still be blindsided by old patterns. But now, you don't meet them with shame or silence. You meet them with breath. With presence. With support. With a body that remembers how to return home.

Chapter Summary - From Repair to Reverence

Recovery is not just about staying sober; it's about staying connected. And sometimes, that connection breaks. Whether through relapse, grief, or overwhelm, the body can lose its sense of safety. But this rupture is not the end of the story. It is the invitation to begin again, gently and more honestly than before.

In this chapter, we explored relapse not as a failure but as a signal. A moment when the nervous system reached for the only form of regulation it knew. When we shift the lens from shame to somatic, we see that the return to substances is often rooted in the return of old patterns, patterns that live in the body, not just the mind. And if the body holds the wound, it also holds the way through.

We learned that somatic relapse repair begins with presence, not punishment. That healing is not about starting over but about staying with ourselves through the mess. And that the nervous system doesn't heal through control; it heals through trust.

As we close this chapter, we open the door to something deeper than repair. We step into reverence for the body, for our stories, and for the sacred experiences that continue to unfold as we learn to stay present. Whether your path is rooted in the 12 Steps, therapy, nature, or your own intuition, the question becomes: *What does it feel like to be held by something larger than yourself?*

In the next chapter, we explore the wisdom that lives not just in belief systems but in your cells. We turn toward spirituality as something embodied, not thought about, but felt. Through breath, through stillness, through movement and emotion, we ask: What if your body was already the temple? What if the divine was never outside of you but waiting within?

Let's walk together, not just away from what once hurt but toward what now heals.

16

EMBODIED SPIRITUALITY - GOD, THE BODY, AND THE SOUL

WHEN GOD ISN'T WHAT YOU THOUGHT

For many of us, the word "God" lands like a punch. It brings back memories of being judged, rejected, or told who we were wasn't enough. Some of us walked away from religion at an early age. Others stayed and silently suffered. So when we arrive at the Steps and see the word "God" staring back at us, we tense up. We brace. And we wonder: *Can I recover if I don't believe?*

The answer is yes. The Steps do not demand belief in a specific God. They ask us to consider that there may be something: a presence, a principle, a rhythm greater than our isolated will. Somatically, this isn't about theology. It's about what happens in your body when you feel supported, when you let go, when you soften. That's spiritual. That's sacred. And for many of us, that's enough.

Jim's Story

"The first time I heard 'God' in a meeting, my stomach clenched so hard I thought I'd throw up. It felt like being twelve again, sitting in church, knowing I didn't belong. But something kept me there. A woman shared about her Higher Power being the sound of the ocean. I could feel something

shift in my chest. My breath slowed. My fists unclenched. I didn't believe in God, but I started believing in moments like that, where I didn't have to fight."

Spirituality can be as simple as the breath that returns after panic. The exhale that whispers, "You're safe now." It can be the sky at dusk, the sound of a friend's voice, or the warmth in your chest when you speak your truth and aren't abandoned. These moments invite us into something bigger, not necessarily a deity, but a felt sense of connection that says: *You're not alone. You're held.*

THE BODY AS THE TEMPLE

We were taught to seek the sacred outside ourselves, in buildings, books, and figures of authority. But what if the temple was always within? What if the body, with all its trembling and healing, its aches and wisdom, was the holiest place we've ever known?

Somatic spirituality begins with presence. It says: come home to your breath, your pulse, your pain. Comes home to the place where your story still lives. This is not about escaping the body to reach some higher state; it's about descending into it to find the divine that's already there.

Every time we slow down to feel what's alive in us, we are practicing devotion. Every time we breathe through discomfort instead of bypassing it, we are bowing at the altar of truth. In recovery, our body becomes the sacred text. It tells the truth even when our minds cannot. It shows us where we're gripping, where we're grieving, and, if we listen, where we're ready to be free.

Faith as a Felt Sense

Faith isn't always belief. Sometimes faith is the courage to stay in your body when everything in you wants to run. Sometimes it's choosing to breathe instead of dissociate. Sometimes, it's taking the next right action without knowing how things will turn out.

In somatic work, this is referred to as *titration*, which involves staying with just enough discomfort to build resilience without overwhelming your system. Faith works the same way. You don't need to leap. You just need to lean. Into your breath. Into a friend. Into a Higher Power you don't have to understand to trust.

Malik's Story

"My sponsor told me to pause before calling my dealer. Just pause. That was it. The first time I tried, my body shook. I thought I was going to crawl out of my skin. But I'd started seeing a somatic therapist who showed me how to track sensation. I found one small place in my body that felt still: my left hand. I stayed there. I breathed. I didn't make the call. That's the moment I started to understand what faith could feel like."

For some, that Higher Power is nature. For others, it's community. For others still, it's the quiet voice inside that says, "**Don't pick up the drink today.**" Whatever it is, it doesn't need to fit a mold. It just needs to help you feel more whole.

BECOMING A VESSEL

As we deepen into embodied spirituality, we stop striving to be spiritual and start allowing ourselves to be vessels for something sacred. We stop trying to perform belief and instead make space for awe. This is what Step Eleven prepares us for: conscious contact, not just with a God "out there," but with the divine intelligence moving through us.

You know this state. It's when you speak from the heart and surprise yourself with the truth that emerges. It's when you're present for someone else's pain and feel no need to fix it, only to witness it. It's when your sobriety stops being about fear and becomes an offering of peace.

Embodied spirituality doesn't require purity, perfection, or piety. It requires presence. Humility. Curiosity. And the willingness to let your body become a living, breathing channel for love, for healing, for connection. You don't have to be religious to carry that light. You just have to be real.

A Spirituality That Stays

In the end, embodied spirituality is about finding something that stays. A center. A pulse. A rhythm you can return to when everything else feels lost. For many of us in recovery, that center was missing for a long time. We outsourced it to substances, to approval, to fantasy. Now, we're building it from within.

Somatic Moment

Try this: Place your hand on your heart. Feel the rise and fall. You don't need to change anything. Just notice. That's your rhythm. That's your returning. That's your God, right there. Not in the sky. Not in the sanctuary. But under your skin, reminding you: I'm still here. And I'm not going anywhere.

This is not the kind of spirituality that collapses under pressure. It's not performative. It's practiced. It's earned. Breath by breath. Boundary by boundary. Truth by truth.

It says: I don't have to know everything to trust. I don't have to understand everything to heal. And I don't have to fix everything to be free.

This is the God of my body. The God that doesn't need a name. The one I feel when I stay.

And this is the soul I'm learning to live from, awake, aware, and finally at home.

Chapter Summary – The Body as a Spiritual Home

Chapter 15 explores the heart of somatic spirituality, the idea that the sacred isn't something we ascend to but something we *return to* through the body. For those of us whose ideas of "God" were shaped by shame or rejection, spirituality in recovery can feel impossible. But in the language of somatics, God doesn't have to mean a deity. It can mean Safety. Stillness. Connection. Truth.

By reframing faith as a *felt sense*, we cultivate the courage to stay with discomfort, the breath that brings us back, and the moment of pause before reaction. This understanding allows us to recognize that spirituality is not about performance. It's presence.

The stories in this chapter illustrate that transformation doesn't always come from belief; it often comes from embodiment. From learning to stay, feel, breathe, and witness what arises without shame.

As we move forward into **Chapter 16: Healing in Real Time**, we'll leave behind theory and step into practice. This next chapter explores what this work looks like in practice, in the body, in relationships, during relapse, and in resilience. These are stories from the front lines of recovery, where sobriety and safety are not abstract concepts but lived, messy, embodied truths.

17

HEALING IN REAL TIME - PERSONAL JOURNEYS OF SOBRIETY AND SAFETY

Matt's Story: I Didn't Know What Safety Felt Like

I didn't get sober on my first try or my fifth. Or my tenth. My name is Matt, and I've been in more detoxes than I can count. I've woken up on gurneys, in police stations, in motel rooms with no idea how I got there. I've had blood in my vomit and shakes so bad I couldn't hold a toothbrush. I've had people who loved me cry, beg, and finally walk away. And still, I drank.

People thought I didn't care. But I did. I cared so much it hurt. The truth is, I wasn't drinking to party anymore. I was drinking to escape the war inside my own body.

Even when I wasn't drinking, I wasn't free. My nervous system was locked in a state of permanent fight-or-flight. My shoulders lived up by my ears. My gut never unclenched. My sleep was broken. I couldn't sit still or stand to be alone. The chaos was constant. And when life hit, an argument, a bill, a memory, I'd break. Not because I wanted to drink but because I didn't have the capacity to stay with what I was feeling. I didn't know what safety felt like.

Relapse, for me, wasn't a failure of willpower. It was my body screaming: "I can't hold this alone."

Everything changed when I met a somatic therapist. She didn't ask what I was thinking; she asked what I was feeling and where. She didn't tell me to push through the craving; she asked if I could notice it without judging it. She invited me to stay with the sensation without running from it. I told her I wanted to bolt. She said, "Can you let your legs feel that urge to run, and just stay?" I cried. For the first time, I wasn't being fixed. I was being felt.

It took months before I could breathe without clenching. My jaw was like iron. But I started learning to pause. To orient to the room when panic hit. To feel my feet. To track the heat in my chest or the shaking in my hands without freaking out. And in those small moments, something inside me whispered, "You're not dying, you're feeling."

That became the heart of my sobriety. Not white-knuckling it, but learning to stay. Sobriety didn't come from some big breakthrough. It came from a thousand moments where I didn't abandon myself.

Today, I've been sober for over a year. For me, that's not just a milestone; it's a miracle. Because now I'm not just sober. I'm alive. I'm present. I'm not trying to escape my body anymore. I'm learning to live in it. For the first time, I trust that I can stay.

Sarah's Story: Relearning Safety After Survival

Sarah's story doesn't begin with drinking; it begins with silence. Two years into sobriety, she still couldn't sleep through the night. Her jaw clenched, shoulders braced, and heart raced. Her nervous system was still wired for war. That's because, for a decade, Sarah served as an Army medic. She had lived through mortar rounds, roadside bombs, and endless nights on high alert.

The war had ended. Her tour was over. But her body hadn't gotten the memo.

Alcohol had been her momentary ceasefire. It was the one thing that could quiet the alarms in her body. When she got sober, the volume returned. She didn't feel better. She felt like a live wire.

Sarah tried talk therapy. She could explain the trauma, describe the flashbacks, and even outline the battlefield. But none of that touched the sheer panic she felt standing in line at the grocery store or hearing a door slam.

The breakthrough came not in insight but in practice.

Her somatic work began small, so small it seemed pointless. Orienting to the room. Naming colors. Noticing shapes. Letting her eyes land on something soothing. She carried smooth stones in her pocket. She touched the wall to remind herself she wasn't back in Iraq. Slowly, her body began to learn that it didn't have to brace.

With time, she could track the flutter in her chest without bolting. She could recognize the clench in her jaw as a signal, not a command. The goal wasn't calm. It was a choice. Could she stay? Could she soften?

Now, more than two years sober, Sarah doesn't say she's cured. She says she's practicing. Practicing presence. Practicing trust. Practicing safety, not in theory, but in her skin.

"I didn't need someone to tell me I was safe," she says. "I needed to *feel* safe. And now, I do. Not always. But enough."

James's Story: Stillness Was the Scariest Thing

Stillness nearly broke James. Not detox. Not withdrawal. Not the shame. Just sitting still.

For six years, James lived outside. Under bridges. In alleys. In abandoned stairwells. Constant movement had kept him alive. Stillness meant danger.

When he got into treatment, sitting in a chair in group therapy triggered a flood of panic. His legs twitched. His hands searched for escape. His eyes checked the exits every 30 seconds.

But his counselor didn't push him to calm down. She said something that stuck: "Stillness isn't safe until your body says it is."

James started his somatic work in motion. Rocking. Tapping. Pacing in rhythm. Slowly, gently, he found his nervous system could tolerate a moment of stillness—then two. Eventually, he managed to last five minutes without checking the door.

"I cried the first time I realized I wasn't under threat," he said. "That I could be still and survive."

Now, James is almost two years sober. He still taps his thighs when anxious. He still moves through cravings with rhythm. But his mornings begin in stillness, feet on the floor, eyes on the light coming through the window.

Sobriety didn't come from conquering stillness. It came from learning that stillness could hold him.

Lena's Story: The First Time I Felt Safe in My Body

Lena's healing didn't begin with sobriety. It began the first time someone asked her, "Can you feel your feet?"

She couldn't. Not then.

By the time she got sober, Lena had survived childhood sexual abuse, teenage dissociation, and a decade of numbing with alcohol. Her body had become a ghost ship, functional but vacant. Alcohol gave her one thing she couldn't get anywhere else: sensation.

Sobriety shattered that. With nothing to mute the trauma, her body roared back to life in flashbacks and night sweats. She almost quit recovery, not because she missed drinking, but because she couldn't bear to feel everything again.

Her somatic therapist didn't ask for a trauma narrative. She asked for a present-moment one. Could Lena feel her hands? Her feet? The rug under her toes? Could she name a color in the room?

The answer was usually no. But then, someday, it was yes.

Lena's somatic healing began with tiny, repeated gestures: holding a mug, tracing the edge of a cushion, and making eye contact without looking away. These were the first safe touches, the first safe sensations.

Now, Lena says she's not just sober. She's reinhabited. Her body is no longer a haunted house. It's her home.

"I used to think numbness was weakness," she says. "Now I see it as brilliance. My body was never broken. It was waiting for safety."

A THERAPIST'S STORY: BEARING WITNESS THROUGH THE BODY

This story reflects the lived clinical experience of a trauma-informed somatic therapist who has spent over a decade working with individuals in early recovery. The stories throughout this book center on personal experiences; this one offers a unique, professional perspective on how safety, presence, and attunement unfold within the therapy room.

One of my earliest clients in recovery came to me after surviving both childhood abuse and a violent assault just six months before she relapsed after five years of sobriety. She walked in, saying, "I don't want to tell the story. I just want to feel human again." Her body was in constant hyperarousal, frozen eyes, rigid spine, and shallow breathing. When I offered a simple grounding practice, like feeling her feet on the ground, she burst into tears. Not because of the memory. But because it was the first time she'd realized her body was still here, still holding everything.

I've sat across from people like her for years, those whose trauma didn't just come from what happened to them but from how their bodies were forced to endure it alone. Addiction, I've come to understand, is so often the survival strategy of a body that was never safe. The nervous system doesn't crave substances; it craves regulation. Belonging. Relief.

I don't ask clients to retell what they're not ready to say. I don't label their defenses as dysfunction. I ask, "Where do you feel that in your body?" And then we stay with it, not to fix it, but to witness it. Sometimes it's a burning in the chest, sometimes a shaking in the legs, sometimes a hollowness behind the eyes. We name it. We breathe into it. We let the body complete what was once interrupted.

One client once said, "I'm afraid if I feel it, I'll disappear." But with time, she learned that presence doesn't erase pain; it holds it. And being witnessed, truly witnessed, often becomes the repair.

I've seen the moment regulation returns: when someone softens into a chair or exhales for the first time in a session. I've heard the words: "I didn't know I was allowed to feel this."

Recovery isn't just abstinence. It's reclamation. Of breath. Of space. Of the right to feel without drowning.

That's what I've learned. That's what I hold. That's what I offer: one moment, one breath, one body at a time.

Chapter Summary – Healing in Real Time

Recovery isn't theoretical. It's personal. It's raw. It lives in the shaking hands, the sleepless nights, the moments of stillness that feel like war zones. In this chapter, we've stepped into the real-time journeys of people: Matt, Sarah, James, Lena, and the therapist who sits with them in the trenches. These are not stories of perfection. They're stories of presence. Stories of bodies that have been through hell and still found a way to stay.

Matt showed us what it means to fail and return again and again, to find safety not in white-knuckling sobriety but in learning how to feel without fleeing. Sarah taught us that survival physiology doesn't turn off with a decision to stop drinking. It takes time, patience, and embodied courage to unlearn danger and relearn trust. James reminded us that sobriety is more than housing; it's learning to live inside your body after years of being hunted by fear. Lena revealed the power of returning to a body she once had to abandon and how numbness isn't failure; it's brilliance in disguise. The therapist's story brought us behind the scenes into the quiet, sacred work of holding space for people who are rediscovering their capacity to stay.

What all of these journeys share is a truth many overlook: **the body holds the story of addiction, and it must be part of the story of recovery.**

These stories weren't about getting it right. They were about learning how to feel again. To breathe. To stay with the discomfort. To return when every instinct says run. This is what somatic recovery looks like, not a straight line but a spiral. A rhythm. A conversation between sensation and safety, between memory and movement.

And yet, for many of us, **the most tender terrain** in recovery is the moment we slip. The relapse. The fall. The shame spiral. The return to something we swore we'd never do again.

In the next chapter, we will not pathologize relapse; we will bring compassion to it. We will explore what the body is trying to communicate when we pick up after staying sober. We'll look at how shame, dysregulation, and unprocessed trauma pull us back into old patterns and how somatic practices can offer us a way forward without judgment. Because even in relapse, we are not broken. We are being asked to listen more deeply.

We're not here to be perfect.

We're here to keep returning to our breath, our truth, our bodies, and our path.

18

WHEN THE BODY REACHES BACK
– A SOMATIC VIEW OF RELAPSE

For anyone who has been in recovery spaces for a while, the phrase *"Relapse is part of the process"* may sound familiar, perhaps even overused. But what if instead of repeating it, we looked at it differently? What if we understood relapse not as a moral failing, not even as a setback, but as a somatic message?

This chapter isn't here to rehash what relapse is. You know the story. You've either lived it or walked with someone who has. But what often gets left out of that story is what's happening beneath the behavior, in the tissues, in the breath, in the body's memory.

From a somatic lens, relapse is not a sign of weakness; it's an overwhelmed system reaching for the only regulation it remembers. The drink, the drug, the behavior, they weren't choices made in logic; they were responses made in survival. And if we want to interrupt that cycle, we have to understand the body's role in it, not just the brain's.

In this chapter, we'll explore what happens before, during, and after relapse, not just emotionally or psychologically but physiologically. We'll look at how unprocessed trauma can hijack our capacity, how shame silences our reach for support, and how somatic repair offers a way home. A way that doesn't begin with self-blame but with self-contact.

Because relapse doesn't erase the progress we've made. It reveals where the next layer of healing is waiting.

BEFORE THE SLIP: THE SOMATIC STORM NO ONE SEES

Relapse doesn't begin with a drink. It begins in the body.

Long before we pick up, the signals are already there: tight shoulders, shallow breath, clenched jaw, that dull sense of disconnection. Something in us goes quiet. Something in us goes tense. And often, we don't even notice. We think we're just tired. Irritable. Stressed. We tell ourselves we're "fine." But underneath, the body is whispering: *Something doesn't feel safe.*

This is the beginning of the somatic storm, the invisible buildup that leads to the moment we lose our grip.

What makes relapse so confusing is how *sudden* it can seem. One minute we're okay, and the next, we're walking into a liquor store or calling someone we swore we'd never speak to again. However, if we zoom out and view the situation from the body's perspective, we can see the momentum. The tension. The turning away from ourselves in small, cumulative ways.

THE DISCONNECTION PHASE: WHEN THE BODY STOPS SPEAKING SOFTLY

Relapse rarely begins with a drink or a drug. It begins quietly, almost imperceptibly. Long before the craving screams, there's a subtle silence, an internal turning away.

We stop listening to the body.

At first, it's minor: we skip the walk that steadies us. We blow past our morning routine. We numb out to noise or dive into busyness. Maybe we miss a meal. Maybe two. We swap nourishment for caffeine or control. We tell ourselves we're fine, just tired, just busy. But underneath, something's shifting.

We no longer notice that tightness in the chest, the dull ache in the gut, the shallow breath. These aren't random symptoms. They're messages. Warnings. Pleas. The body whispers first. But when we don't listen, it gets louder. And if we still don't listen, it shuts down.

This isn't a weakness or failure. This is a nervous system under siege, doing what it must to survive. Trauma trains the body to disconnect as a form of protection. In the face of overload, disconnection can feel safer than feeling. So we "power through." We hold our breath. We smile when we want to scream. We stay too long in conversations that hurt, in environments that drain, in expectations that choke.

This is the phase of subtle erosion. Where attunement fades, and automaticity takes its place. Where the present moment becomes something to escape, not inhabit. This is not yet a relapse, but it is the soil in which it grows.

Here, in this phase, we need tenderness, not shame. The nervous system isn't betraying us; it's trying to cope. The tragedy is not the disconnection itself; it's when we don't notice it happening. Or worse, when we notice and judge ourselves for it.

But what if we could pause here? What if we could feel the drift and respond with compassion? What if we could return before the collapse?

Relapse doesn't start with a decision. It starts with disembodiment. And recovery isn't just about abstinence; it's about remembering how to *stay* with ourselves.

Somatic Practice: Two-Minute Body Check

Set a timer for two minutes. Sit somewhere quiet. Close your eyes or lower your gaze. Ask yourself:

- *What am I feeling in my jaw?*
- *What's the weight of my shoulders?*

- *Can I feel my feet touching the ground?*
- *Am I breathing into my belly or holding my breath?*

You don't need to change anything. Just notice. Let your attention come home to your body.

This is how we interrupt the drift.

THE INTERNAL PRESSURE COOKER: WHEN THE BODY CAN'T HOLD IT ALL

After disconnection comes compression. The body, no longer in dialogue with itself, begins to hold everything in. This is where the tension builds: quietly, relentlessly.

Unprocessed emotions, unmet needs, and unsaid truths don't disappear. They settle in the tissues. They gather weight in the chest, in the gut, in the throat. For many of us, the body becomes a silent pressure cooker, trying to metabolize pain we've never been taught how to hold.

When life moves too fast or when echoes from the past resurface without warning, we brace. We tighten. We say, *"I've got it,"* when really, we're barely hanging on.

Support may be available, but we don't reach for it. Not because we don't want help but because old survival patterns whisper, *"Don't be a burden. Don't show weakness. Handle it alone."* So we isolate. We distract. We overwork. We scroll. We over-control. And beneath it all, the internal pressure mounts.

This isn't just anxiety. It's somatic overflow. It's what happens when the body is carrying too much, too fast, with nowhere to place it.

We might feel it as restlessness. Agitation. A short fuse. A creeping sense that something bad is just around the corner. The nervous system is trying to warn us: *"I'm overwhelmed."* But it has no words, only sensations. And because these sensations can feel intolerable, we look for ways to escape them. We don't always know we're doing it.

But the brain starts scanning for relief. The same relief that once came from a substance, a behavior, a coping mechanism we thought we'd left behind.

This is a critical juncture. One that doesn't require discipline; it requires *containment*. Co-regulation. A space to exhale. The question isn't *"How do I make this go away?"* but *"What does my body need in order to release what it's holding?"*

Because the craving, when it comes, won't be random. It will be an attempt to lower the pressure.

For many of us, the body holds unresolved trauma like a silent pressure. When something in our day, or our past, feels too big, too fast, or too uncertain, we brace. We disconnect from others. We might isolate, ruminate, or distract. All the while, the internal tension builds. We feel it as restlessness, agitation, a sense that *something bad is coming*.

This is the body trying to process too much, too quickly, without enough support.

Somatic Practice: Naming Your State

Pause and name your current state gently:

- *"I feel tight."*
- *"I feel numb."*
- *"I feel like running."*

By naming it without judgment, we create just enough space between the state and the spiral.

Awareness is the first step to regulation.

EARLY CRAVING AS A CALL FOR CONTACT

Cravings don't always announce themselves with urgency. Sometimes, it slips in like a thought. A whisper. A "what if." It's easy to mistake it for a desire to use, but often, it's a longing to *feel okay*.

What we call craving is often the body's cry for connection and regulation. It's not just a chemical hunger. It's the nervous system, dysregulated and desperate, reaching for anything that once brought the illusion of calm. Alcohol, or any addictive behavior, becomes the shortcut. Not because we want to self-destruct but because we want to *feel less alone inside ourselves.*

When the inner world feels like too much, too loud, too fast, too full of ache, the drink doesn't seem like a mistake. It feels like mercy.

In that moment, the brain remembers the numbing, the slowing, the soft blur alcohol once provided. It doesn't remember the fallout. It remembers the pause. The brief exhale. The false sense of safety.

This is the most misunderstood part of the relapse cycle. Craving isn't always about wanting to escape. Sometimes, it's about trying to come home to our own bodies without knowing how. But here's the truth: that longing, that ache underneath the craving, is a doorway. It's not asking for discipline. It's asking for *presence*. For contact. For breath, for stillness, for safe connection, either with another person or with ourselves.

The craving is a signal, not a failing. If we can pause and ask, *"What am I really needing right now?"* we begin to turn toward healing rather than away from it.

The relief that substances offer is real, but it's fleeting. And the cost is not just physical; it's relational, emotional, and spiritual. Every time we override the body's call for connection with a substitute, the deeper need goes unmet. But every time we respond with compassion, we build a new pathway. One that doesn't end in collapse but in reconnection.

Somatic Practice: Contact and Grounding

In a moment of agitation, place one hand on your chest and one hand on your belly. Feel the warmth of your touch. Then, place both feet firmly on the ground and push gently down through the soles.

Whisper to yourself: *"I'm here. I'm still here."*

This simple act reconnects you to yourself, body to breath, presence to place.

The Collapse: When the Body Says "Enough"

Collapse doesn't always look dramatic. Sometimes, it looks like silence. Like staying in bed too long. Missing a meeting. Ignoring a call. Sometimes, it's a quiet giving-up, not because we want to relapse, but because we've run out of nervous system capacity to fight it.

By this point, the body is no longer whispering. It has tried to signal through fatigue, tension, cravings, and disconnection. Now, it goes offline.

Collapse is what happens when the pressure has built up too long without relief. The body, overwhelmed and unregulated, can no longer hold the tension of survival without a release valve. So it folds in on itself. This is the shutdown. The freeze. The blankness.

For many, this is when the relapse happens, not as a conscious betrayal of recovery but as an act of nervous system triage. The drink, the binge, the fix, and the escape aren't about pleasure. It's about *relief*. It's about making the unbearable bearable, even just for a moment.

What's important to understand here is that this phase is not a moral failure. It is a physiological threshold. The body is exhausted from carrying too much, too alone, for too long. And yet, this moment holds the potential for radical compassion.

Because collapse, while painful, is honest. It reveals what we could not sustain. It shows us the point where we needed support but didn't, or couldn't, reach for it. This is not the end of the story. It's the moment when the nervous system asks, "*Can you hold me now?*" "*Even here?*" "*Even after this?*"

Recovery is not about never collapsing. It's about learning how to return. How to re-engage, slowly, gently, from the inside out.

If you find yourself here, in the stillness after the storm, the shame after the slip, pause. Breathe. You are not broken. You are not starting over. You are continuing. Healing isn't linear, and collapse doesn't erase the progress you've made. It's a message, not a verdict.

The question now is not, *"Why did I fall?"* but *"What was I carrying alone?"*

And *"What might be possible if I no longer had to?"*

What Collapse Feels Like

Collapse doesn't always feel dramatic. It can feel numb. Flat. Blank. Like the color drains from the day.

You might feel like you're watching life happen from the outside. Like everything is muffled. Your body feels heavy, your mind foggy. It's hard to make decisions, sometimes even small ones, like what to eat, shower, or answer a text. There's a sense of disconnection not just from others but from yourself.

Some describe it as feeling like they're "underwater" or "in a cave." Others feel frozen like they want to move, reach out, and cry but can't.

It's not laziness. It's not weakness. It's a nervous system that has exceeded its threshold and gone into energy conservation mode. You may feel deep fatigue but can't rest. You may want comfort but feel unreachable. You may crave help but feel ashamed to ask for it.

And all of that is understandable. Because collapse is not chosen, it's automatic. It's the body's last-ditch effort to survive what it perceives as too much.

Somatic Practice: Post-Trigger Pause (Even Mid-Spiral)

If you find yourself mid-collapse, the body can still be reached.

Try this: stop. Press your feet into the ground. Even if you've already relapsed, press down gently.

Can you feel the floor? Can you feel the support beneath you?

Bring one hand to your chest. If it's shaking, let it. If it's numb, notice that too.

You're still here. You're still in a body. You are not lost.

This practice is not to stop the spiral. It's to stay with yourself inside it.

What Collapse Feels Like

Collapse doesn't always feel dramatic. It can feel numb. Flat. Blank. Like the color drains from the day.

You might feel like you're watching life happen from the outside. Like everything is muffled. Your body feels heavy, your mind foggy. It's hard to make decisions—sometimes even small ones like what to eat, whether to shower, or whether to answer a text. There's a sense of disconnection not just from others but from yourself.

Some describe it as feeling like they're "underwater" or "in a cave." Others feel frozen, like they want to move, reach out, cry, but can't.

It's not laziness. It's not weakness. It's a nervous system that has exceeded its threshold and gone into energy conservation mode. You may feel deep fatigue, but can't rest. You may want comfort but feel unreachable. You may crave help but feel ashamed to ask for it.

And all of that is understandable. Because collapse is not chosen—it's automatic. It's the body's last-ditch effort to survive what it perceives as too much.

THE REPAIR PHASE: RECONNECTING AFTER THE STORM

Repair doesn't mean fixing what's broken. It means reweaving what was frayed. Returning to the body not with judgment but with gentleness.

The first step in repair is *slowness*. After a collapse, your nervous system is tender. Overstretched. It doesn't need plans or promises; it needs presence. A sip of water. A soft blanket. A walk. A moment of safe eye contact. Small acts of kindness toward your body help signal, *"We're not in danger anymore."*

Repair may look different each time. Sometimes it's reaching out to someone who won't shame you. Sometimes it's lying on the floor with your hand on your belly, just breathing. Sometimes it's simply naming what happened, not to spiral in guilt, but to understand the sequence.

This phase is where integration begins. You begin to trace the breadcrumbs that led to collapse, not to punish yourself but to learn what the body was trying to say along the way.

Ask yourself:

- Where did I disconnect?
- What was I carrying alone?
- What did I need that I didn't know how to ask for?
- What helped, even just a little?

Repair is less about what you *do* and more about how you *relate* to yourself. Can you be curious instead of critical? Can you offer warmth instead of war?

Every return to the body strengthens your resilience. Every compassionate repair teaches your nervous system *even when we fall; we can find our way home.*

And that's the real work of recovery, not perfection, but reconnection.

AFTER THE FALL: SHAME, SHUTDOWN, AND THE SILENCE THAT FOLLOWS

After relapse, many people disappear from meetings, from therapists, and from friends. This silence is not apathy. It's *protection*. It's a nervous system trying to shield itself from rejection.

But silence feeds shame. And shame keeps us stuck.

The body needs connection without correction most after a fall—someone who can sit beside us, breathe with us, and say, *"You still belong."*

A stillness settles in, not the kind that soothes, but the kind that suffocates. The body folds inward. The mind loops. And what fills the space is not just regret but shame, a deep, embodied sense of "*I am wrong,*" not just "*I did wrong.*"

Shame can be deceptive. It doesn't always scream. Sometimes it whispers through your posture, the slump of your shoulders, the way your eyes won't meet a mirror. It silences your voice, pulls you away from connection, and convinces you that you're alone again.

This is the shutdown phase. It's not just emotional; it's physiological. The nervous system, already under strain, has now reached a state of collapse. You may feel numb, flattened, disconnected from your body and sense of worth. You may avoid others, not because you want to be alone, but because you're afraid your pain will be met with judgment instead of care.

This is when the old voices get loud:

"You blew it."

"No one will understand."

"Start over. Try harder."

But in somatic healing, we do not start over; we start ***again*** with deeper awareness and greater compassion.

This moment is sacred. Not because it feels good but because it's a chance to unlearn the shame-based cycle that relapse often reinforces. Your relapse is not a betrayal of your recovery. It's information. It's the body asking for help in the only way it knows how. It's a moment that requires you to turn *toward* yourself, not away.

The question isn't: *"How do I punish myself into sobriety?"*

The question is: *"How can I repair with my body, my breath, and my being?"*

Repairing the Body's Trust: A Somatic Exercise for Post-Relapse Return

Before you move forward, give your body a place to land. What follows is a simple, powerful somatic exercise designed to support reconnection, containment, and gentle self-regulation after relapse or emotional overwhelm.

Exercise: Ground and Return (5–7 Minutes)

Find a Safe Space

Sit or lie down in a quiet place where you won't be interrupted. Let your body settle without forcing stillness.

Orient to the Room

Gently move your eyes around the space. Name 3–5 things you can see. Feel your spine in the chair or your back on the floor. Remind yourself: *I am here. I am safe enough in this moment.*

Hand-to-Heart, Hand-to-Belly

Place one hand on your chest and the other on your lower belly. Close your eyes if that feels safe. Feel the temperature, the weight, the contact. Let your body feel *held.*

Breathe Low and Slow

Inhale through your nose for a count of 4.

Exhale through your mouth for a count of 6.

Let the exhale be long, soft, and complete. Repeat this breath for several rounds. Imagine the exhale releasing tension from your shoulders, your jaw, and your gut.

A Healing Phrase

When ready, speak softly, aloud, or silently:

"I am allowed to begin again. My body remembers healing. I can return."

Close with Contact

Before ending, place both hands over your heart and say thank you to your body, not for being perfect, but for surviving. For staying. For being here.

This is not about fixing yourself. This is about *being with yourself* in the aftermath. With care. With truth. With breath.

Bridging to What Comes Next

Relapse is not a single event; it's a series of nervous system shifts that begin long before a drink or drug re-enters the picture. In this chapter, we explored the whole arc: from subtle disconnection and internal pressure to craving, collapse, and the silence that often follows. We reframed relapse not as a failure but as a physiological and emotional threshold that calls for compassion, repair, and reconnection. Most importantly, we began to see relapse not as an endpoint but as a message from the body: *I need more safety, more support, more care.*

That message often begins with a **trigger**.

In Chapter 18, we'll look closely at what triggers really are, not just emotional reactions but somatic warning signs of overwhelm. Whether it's a sound, a memory, a tone of voice, or a subtle shift in someone else's energy, a trigger can send the body back into old survival patterns. When we don't understand how to recognize or respond to these cues, they often lead us right back to relapse. But when we learn to notice them—early, compassionately, we can interrupt the cycle. We can choose safety instead of shutdown.

Let's begin there.

19

BOUNDARIES, TRIGGERS, AND SAFETY

By now, you've learned that relapse doesn't happen in a single moment; it builds. And what often goes unnoticed in that build-up is how much we override our inner signals. We push through discomfort. We ignore red flags. We stay too long in unsafe environments or conversations. And we call it strength.

But true strength in recovery comes from protection, not from armor, but from *attunement*. That's what this chapter is about: learning how to recognize what overwhelms your system and how to respond with boundaries, awareness, and self-respect. Because safety isn't a luxury; it's a *requirement* for healing.

Let's begin with a truth many of us never got to hear growing up: The Nervous System Craves Safety, Not Control

- Reframes boundaries and trigger responses as *biological needs*, not emotional weaknesses.
- Explains that trauma survivors often mistake control for safety and how somatic safety redefines that.

"We don't need more discipline. We need more internal containment. That's what safety actually is."

THE NERVOUS SYSTEM CRAVES SAFETY, NOT CONTROL

When we've lived through trauma, chaos, or addiction, we often confuse control with safety. We try to control people, schedules, substances, or feelings because we believe that if we can *just manage everything*, we'll finally feel okay.

But control doesn't equal regulation. In fact, it often pulls us further away from our bodies.

Somatically speaking, what your nervous system craves is not control but *containment*. Containment is internal safety. It's the felt sense that *I can be with what's happening without being overwhelmed by it.*

Here's the key difference:

- **Control** is external. It focuses on manipulating what's *out there* to create a sense of safety.
- **Containment** is internal. It helps us regulate what's *in here* so we can face life with steadiness.

Think about early sobriety: how often did you white-knuckle through situations, trying to look strong while your insides were screaming? That wasn't healing. That was surviving. And it's okay; we did what we had to do. But now, we're learning a new way.

We don't need more discipline. We need more *containment*.

Containment comes from learning the language of your nervous system. It's what happens when you set a boundary, and your breath deepens. When you step out of a triggering space and your muscles unclench. When you say *no* and feel your chest soften. These moments don't just protect your sobriety; they *rebuild your relationship with your body.*

You don't have to be in control of everything to be okay.

You just need to be in a relationship with *yourself.*

UNDERSTANDING TRIGGERS: WHAT THEY REALLY ARE

We hear the word *trigger* so often in recovery it's easy to forget what it means.

A trigger isn't just a bad memory or a painful reminder; it's a nervous system event. It's your body reacting to something it *perceives* as dangerous, even if that danger isn't happening right now.

You could be in a safe room with safe people and still feel like the walls are closing in. That's not irrational. That's your body remembering before your brain can catch up.

Triggers are biological. They live in the body, not just in the mind. They can be set off by sights, sounds, smells, words, tones of voice, or even internal sensations. The reaction is often instant and automatic; before you even know what's happening, your heart is racing, your breath is shallow, and you want to escape.

When you're triggered, your nervous system shifts into a survival state: fight, flight, freeze, or fawn. You may feel the urge to lash out or shut down completely. You might dissociate, people-please, get flooded with shame, or suddenly crave a drink and not know why.

This is *not* weakness. It's the body doing what it was trained to do: survive threat.

But healing begins when we stop judging the reaction and start noticing it.

Trigger Symptoms Checklist

Notice how your body responds when you're triggered:

- ☐ Racing heart or pounding chest
- ☐ Shallow, rapid breathing
- ☐ Feeling frozen, paralyzed, or blank
- ☐ Muscle tension (jaw clenching, fists, shoulders)
- ☐ Nausea or tightness in the gut
- ☐ Sweaty palms or hot face

- ☐ Tunnel vision or sense of "leaving your body"
- ☐ Sudden urge to escape, shut down, or use a substance
- ☐ Flood of emotion that feels bigger than the moment

You don't have to feel all of these; just one can signal your system is activated.

Recognizing your triggers doesn't mean you've failed. It means your body is working and asking for your attention. The goal isn't to eliminate every trigger. It's to build enough regulation to move through them without losing yourself.

The Sacred Pause: What to Do *Before* You React

Most relapses don't begin in the moment someone picks up a drink, pops a pill, or reaches out to the person they swore they'd block. They begin in the *nervous system*, quietly, subtly, and often invisibly. They begin hours, days, or even weeks earlier in the overwhelm that goes unacknowledged. In the breath that stays stuck in the chest. In the tightening jaw you ignore, the fatigue you override, the rising panic you smile through.

They begin when something inside says, *"This is too much."*

Too much stimulation.

Too much silence.

Too much pain, too fast, with too little support.

That's the spiral, when your body senses a threat but doesn't yet have the tools to respond safely. And for trauma survivors, that's not a psychological glitch; it's a survival reflex. The very places where we were once powerless get lit up again, and without grounding, without containment, the next move often isn't a conscious choice—it's an attempt to escape.

This is why the ***pause*** is not just a coping skill. It's a *somatic intervention*. A moment where we place space between the *trigger* and the *reaction*, not to suppress it, but to stay *with ourselves* in the moment we're most tempted to leave.

The pause is where the nervous system gets to ask:

"Am I safe?"

"Am I alone?"

"Can I choose differently?"

The pause isn't passive. It's an act of self-protection. It's a reclamation of agency in a body that once survived by shutting down, acting out, or going numb.

This is the heartbeat of somatic recovery.

You don't push through the trigger.

You *meet yourself inside it.*

And in doing so, you create the possibility of something trauma never gave you: **choice.**

The Pause Protocol (Somatic Tool)

This simple 4-step practice can stop the spiral before it becomes a relapse:

1. Name It

Say—out loud if possible—*"I'm triggered."*

Naming it breaks the trance. It tells your nervous system: "I see you." "I'm here."

2. Locate It

Ask: *Where in my body is this showing up?*

Chest tightness? Jaw clenching? Gut ache? Fuzzy head? Simply noticing it starts to ground you.

3. Take 3 Regulating Breaths

Inhale through the nose (count to 4), exhale slowly through the mouth (count to 6).

Let the exhale be soft and complete. Do this three times. Watch your system begin to settle.

4. Delay Action

Wait 5 to 15 minutes before taking any action. This window gives your body time to downshift.

Walk outside. Hold a cold cloth. Stretch. Call someone. Don't *react*. Just *be*.

"The pause is not passive. It's the most powerful decision you can make with a dysregulated body."

The HALT Check-In

One of the simplest yet most powerful tools I return to again and again is something I learned early in my recovery: **HALT**.

It stands for **Hungry, Angry, Lonely, Tired**, and it's not just a mental checklist. It's a direct map back to the body.

So often, when we feel like we're spiraling, anxious, foggy, emotionally flooded, it's not because something is wrong with us. It's because something *basic* is missing. The body is trying to communicate a need, and when that need is ignored, it gets louder and more urgent. If we don't pause to listen, that urgency often turns into craving.

Next time you feel overwhelmed or like something's just *off*, gently bring awareness inward and ask:

HUNGRY – What does my body need for nourishment right now?

This isn't just about food. It's about fuel, grounding, energy.

Did I skip a meal? Did I eat something nourishing or just sugar and caffeine? Is my body weak or depleted?

Place a hand on your belly. Breathe. Ask, *"What kind of support do I need physically?"*

ANGRY – What am I holding in that needs space or voice?

Anger is energy. And when it's trapped in the body, it simmers as tension—tight shoulders, clenched jaw, racing thoughts.

Have I swallowed my truth today? Am I carrying resentment, irritation, or frustration without release?

Feel your fists—are they tight? Your chest—does it feel hot or closed? That's the body asking for expression.

LONELY – Where am I feeling disconnected or unseen?

Loneliness doesn't just mean being physically alone. It's a state of emotional and energetic disconnection.

Do I feel isolated? Have I gone too long without meaningful contact? Have I shared honestly with anyone today?

Place your hand on your heart. Notice any ache, heaviness, or emptiness. Let it be there. It's a sign you're ready for connection.

TIRED – Is my body or spirit calling for rest?

Tired doesn't always mean sleepy—it can mean emotionally saturated, overextended, or on the verge of collapse.

Have I been over-functioning? Pushing past my limits? Ignoring my body's signals to slow down?

Lie down. Close your eyes for a moment. Let your body settle without fixing or doing. Ask, *"Is it safe to rest right now?"*

Relapse doesn't begin with a bottle or a binge. It often begins when we override these *basic* somatic signals.

The HALT check-in is a way of gently and truthfully returning to what your body is asking for *before* the craving arises.

Sometimes, healing means simply feeding yourself.

Or naming your anger.

Or reaching out.

Or going to bed early.

These are not small things. They are *recovery in action*.

A Story from the Author

There was a night, early in my recovery, when the craving didn't come loudly. It crept in like a fog. I couldn't name it at first. I was pacing. My breath was shallow. My shoulders were tight and creeping toward my ears. I felt irritable and disconnected but had no idea why. All I knew was that something in me wanted *out*.

I almost reached for my old habits, the text, the rum, the escape. But instead, I paused. I sat on the floor, closed my eyes, and checked in. Not just mentally but *somatically*. I asked myself: "*Where is this living in my body?*" "*What am I actually feeling?*"

Then I ran through the **HALT** check-in:

- **Hungry** – I hadn't eaten all day. My stomach felt hollow. No wonder I was so shaky.
- **Angry** – I had just kept the peace in a hard conversation. My throat felt tight; I hadn't said what I needed to.
- **Lonely** – I hadn't talked to anyone real all day. I'd been performing, not connecting.
- **Tired** – My eyes burned, and my back was aching from pushing too hard.

I was all four. No wonder my system was dysregulated. It wasn't about the craving; it was about what my body was carrying. And that night, instead of spiraling out of control, I chose to tend to those needs. I fed myself something warm. I moved my body gently. I cried. I reached out. I curled up and let myself *rest*.

That night, I didn't relapse.

Because I paused.

Because I listened.

Because I didn't override my body, I honored it.

HALT isn't just a checklist. It's a call back into the body. And sometimes, that's enough to save us.

BOUNDARY WORK IS RECOVERY WORK

For many of us in recovery, the word *"boundary"* once sounded like punishment. Like walls. Like rejection. But boundaries aren't about pushing others away; they're about drawing a sacred circle around what helps us heal.

In sobriety, *boundaries are not just about saying no to others; they're about saying yes to yourself.* Yes, to safety. Yes, to regulation. Yes, to the version of you that knows chaos is no longer a requirement for love.

Boundaries are how we make sobriety *liveable*. And in somatic recovery, they don't just live in language; they live in the body.

Somatic Boundaries: Your Body Knows the Line

You don't always need words to know when a boundary is being crossed.

Sometimes your body tells you first.

- That tightening in your throat when someone speaks over you? A sign.
- That pit in your stomach when a certain topic comes up? A signal.
- That overwhelming fatigue after a phone call? A clue.
- That deep breath and chest expansion when you're with someone safe? That's your *nervous system saying yes*.

Somatic boundaries are the nervous system's way of letting you know:

"This feels safe."

"This feels like too much."

"This is not for me right now."

When we ignore those signals, we don't just risk discomfort; we risk relapse.

Why? Because pushing past your own limits is a form of self-abandonment. And the body remembers every time you didn't listen.

Three Kinds of Boundaries Every Recovering Person Needs

1. Physical Boundaries

This includes your physical space, touch, proximity, and environment. You have the right to say:

- *"I need space right now."*
- *"Please don't touch me without asking."*
- *"I'm not comfortable in that location."*

Pay attention to body cues like tension, flinching, or shrinking away; these are physical indicators that something doesn't feel safe. Trust them.

2. Emotional Boundaries

This is about your inner world, your feelings, values, and personal truth.

You get to decide:

- What topics you're willing to engage in
- What kind of energy you let into your emotional space
- Who gets access to your vulnerability

If a conversation is leaving you emotionally raw or dysregulated, that's a boundary issue, not a weakness. Your tears, anger, or dissociation are signals worth honoring.

3. Energetic Boundaries

Often the most overlooked, these are about your capacity. Your *yes* has limits.

You are allowed to say:

- *"I don't have the capacity for this conversation right now."*
- *"I can't take that on today."*
- *"I need rest."*

If you leave a situation feeling depleted, drained, or spaced out, that's your energy saying: *"I gave too much."* Your recovery depends on your ability to preserve and protect your life force.

Nervous System Awareness Is the Real Boundary

Boundaries aren't just something you speak; they're something you *feel*. Long before a word is said, your nervous system knows when a line has been crossed. It tightens. It contracts. It whispers, *"This doesn't feel safe."*

True boundary work begins in the body.

You don't just protect your sobriety with firm conversations or rigid rules; you protect it by learning to sense when your inner safety is at risk. That's nervous system awareness, and it's the foundation of lasting recovery.

When you begin to build somatic boundaries, you do more than create space from stress or chaos; you send a powerful message to your body:

"I hear you now. I won't leave you behind. I will no longer abandon you to stay in relationships, situations, or patterns that harm us."

That, right there, is the deepest boundary of all.

Building Your Safety Sanctuary

In a world that's often loud, unpredictable, and overwhelming, healing begins with having a space where your nervous system knows it can let go. A place where nothing is demanded of you. Where you don't have to explain, perform, or be anything other than exactly as you are.

For me, this wasn't something I had right away in sobriety. In the beginning, my body didn't know safety. My home didn't feel like a refuge; it just felt like a place where I wasn't drinking. But over time, I realized I needed more than abstinence. I needed sanctuary.

That's when I started creating what I now call my *Safety Sanctuary*, a dedicated space, however small, where I could come back to myself. A space for regulating, restoring, and remembering that I am not in danger anymore.

Your Sanctuary Is Sacred—Not Fancy

You don't need a whole room. You don't need expensive items. You need *intention*.

It could be a corner of your bedroom, a chair by the window, or a spot on the floor with a favorite blanket. What matters is that your body begins to associate this space with safety. I know that for me, I needed something special and felt it was time to pamper myself, so I took a bedroom and transformed it into my own sanctuary.

Here's how to start building your own:

Creating Your Safety Sanctuary: Step by Step

1. Choose Your Spot

Pick a space in your home where you can feel quiet, uninterrupted, and at ease. It doesn't have to be big, just consistent.

Ask your body: "Where do I feel most able to exhale?"

2. Set the Tone with the Senses

Bring in items that speak to your nervous system:

- **Touch**: soft blankets, cushions, stuffed animals, warm socks
- **Sight**: gentle lighting, nature imagery, calming colors
- **Smell**: essential oils, candles, incense, or a familiar scent
- **Sound**: a soothing playlist, wind chimes, nature sounds
- **Temperature**: a cozy heater or cool fan, whatever your body needs to soften

3. Return Often—Not Just in Crisis

This is key: your safety sanctuary isn't just for emergencies. It's for *maintenance*.

Visit it daily if you can. Sit there when you're calm, not just triggered. Let your nervous system learn:

"This is where I go to regulate. This is where I land."

Over time, just stepping into that space will start to send the signal: *You're safe now.*

Somatic Exercise: Creating Your Safety Nest

Try this the first time you sit in your sanctuary space or anytime you need to ground yourself.

1. **Settle** into your space. Get physically comfortable. Close your eyes if it feels safe to do so.
2. **Touch** something soft and grounding, such as a cushion, a blanket, or your own hand.
3. **Breathe** gently in through the nose and out through the mouth. Long, slow exhale.
4. **Visualize** this space wrapping around you like a cocoon. Not to trap you but to hold you.
5. **Place your hands** over your chest or belly and say silently:

"This space belongs to me. This is where I come to feel safe."

1. **Stay for 2–5 minutes** (or longer). Let your body experience the sensation of *rest without fear.*

Creating a safety sanctuary isn't self-indulgent; it's self-regulation in action. It teaches your body that not every place has to feel like a battlefield. That you are allowed to rest, receive, and reconnect. And when you give yourself that gift regularly, you don't just feel safe; you *become* a safe place to live.

Relapse as a Boundary Breach

By now, we've explored how relapse rarely starts in the moment of action; it begins in the body, in the overwhelm, in the silence. But here's something many people in recovery don't realize until later: *relapse is often a sign that a boundary was crossed, one we didn't notice or honor in time.*

Sometimes, *that boundary is physical*:

We stayed too long in a place that didn't feel safe, maybe a loud event, a bar "just to be social," or a toxic home.

Sometimes, *it's emotional*:

We kept smiling while our insides were screaming. We nodded along to keep the peace. We swallowed anger or fear instead of speaking it.

Sometimes, *it's energetic*:

We gave too much. Said yes too many times. Took on someone else's crisis until we collapsed under the weight.

And because we didn't notice the breach or didn't believe we had the right to act on it, our bodies tried to protect us the only way they knew how: through escape. That escape often looked like relapse.

Relapse, in this light, is not just about craving or failure. It's about *self-abandonment*. It's what happens when the nervous system screams, *"This is too much!"* but we've been taught to keep going anyway.

> *"Every relapse I've had was preceded by a moment where I didn't speak up, walk away, or ask for help."*
>
> — M, THE AUTHOR

That statement isn't about blame. It's about awareness. Because if we can trace the moment we overrode our limit, we can learn from it. We can pause next time. We can act sooner. We can protect our sobriety by first protecting our *nervous system.*

Questions to Reflect On (Somatic Boundary Check-In)

If you've had a slip, setback, or full relapse, ask yourself:

- Where did I say yes when I wanted to say no?
- When did my body tell me to leave, and I stayed?
- Who or what drained my energy before the craving hit?
- What conversation, environment, or expectation pushed me past my window of tolerance?
- Did I try to power through instead of pause and regulate?

Your answers are not punishments. They're *permission slips*. They help you recover with more wisdom, not more shame.

Relapse is not the opposite of recovery; it's a message. A boundary was crossed. A need was unmet. Something inside said *"no,"* and we ignored it.

But now, you're learning to listen. You're learning to stay close to the part of you that whispers, *"This doesn't feel right."*

And every time you do, you're not just preventing relapse. You're repairing the deepest boundary of all: the one between *you* and *yourself.*

Your Boundaried Self Is Your Empowered Self

In early recovery, boundaries can feel like barriers. At first, they may bring discomfort, awkwardness, or even guilt. Saying *no*, stepping away, admitting *"this is too much"*—it all feels foreign when trauma taught us to tolerate and adapt instead of protect and preserve.

But with time, boundaries stop feeling like walls—and start feeling like *home*.

Every time you listen to your body and honor its limit, you're not shutting people out—you're *inviting yourself in*. You're saying, *"I matter."*

You're saying, *"I get to feel safe."*

You're saying, *"I'm allowed to be a full human being, not a sponge for other people's energy."*

Boundaries aren't about being rigid or cold. They're about being real. They allow you to live aligned with your values, your capacity, and your nervous system. When you trust your "no," your "yes" becomes more powerful. When you step away from what drains you, you step *toward* what heals you.

You don't just build boundaries to protect your sobriety.

You build boundaries to protect the version of yourself who knows she is finally worth protecting.

That's not selfish. That's *sovereign*.

That's not disconnection. That's **embodied empowerment.**

Chapter Summary

This chapter explored the intimate relationship between nervous system regulation and sobriety. We learned that:

- Triggers are not just memories; they're *body-based alerts* that signal a need for safety.
- The *pause* isn't weakness; it's your most powerful tool for self-regulation.

- HALT is not an acronym; it's an invitation to meet your unmet needs with care.
- Boundaries are not walls; they are *living expressions* of your self-respect, energy, and healing.
- And relapse often isn't about failure; it's what happens when we override our inner limits.

What you're building here isn't just a sober life; it's a regulated life.

A life where you listen before the spiral.

A life where you choose yourself before you abandon yourself.

*A life where **your body gets to be the compass**, not the casualty.*

For many of us, the body hasn't felt like a safe place for a long time. It was where trauma happened. Where shame lived. Where we learned to disconnect in order to survive. But healing asks us to return, to rebuild a new relationship with the very place we once left behind.

In the next chapter, we'll explore what it means to truly trust your body again. Not just to listen to it but to believe it. To work *with* it, not against it. To rebuild safety *from the inside out.*

Because your recovery is not just a journey through the mind; It's a reunion with the body you live in.

20

TRUSTING THE BODY AGAIN

THE BODY WAS NEVER THE ENEMY – IT WAS THE MESSENGER

For a long time, I didn't hate my body, but I didn't trust it either. Mostly, I was tired. Not just physically but *existentially* tired. Soul-tired. Nervous-system-tired. I was tired of waking up already exhausted. Tired of pushing through one more thing. Tired of feeling like my body was always lagging behind where my life demanded it be.

Back then, I thought it was laziness. Or depression. Or maybe I just wasn't built for a "normal" life. I'd get frustrated with myself: *"Why can't I just handle it? Why does everything feel so heavy?"* I was white-knuckling through my days, and when I couldn't muscle my way through anymore, I'd shut down.

Fatigue became the quiet ache beneath everything I did.

But what I see now, what I couldn't have seen then, is this:

That fatigue was never failure. It was my body begging for something different.

Not escape. Not control. But care. Stillness. Safety. Nourishment. Boundaries. And most of all, *attention*. *My body wasn't trying to ruin my life. It was trying to save it.*

Letters to the Body: The Turning Point

I remember the first time I wrote a letter to my body. I was curled up on the floor of my bedroom, feeling like I was failing recovery because I was so tired all the time. Everyone else seemed to be "doing the work," and I was just *lying down*.

But something in me whispered, *"Write."*

So I did.

Dear body,

I'm sorry.

I'm sorry I thought you were the problem.

I'm sorry I only listened when you screamed.

I'm sorry I pushed you, starved you, ignored your shaking and your silence.

You've been trying to protect me from things I never named.

Thank you for not giving up. Thank you for still being here.

I promise, I'm listening now.

Love,

-M

That letter didn't solve everything. But it softened something. For the first time, I wasn't trying to force my body into healing, I was *inviting it back into the conversation.*

Others Learning to Listen

Everyone comes to this moment differently. Some with anger. Some with grief. Some with awe.

Jay, 36 – a lifelong overachiever, wrote:

Dear body,

I bullied you for years.

I called you lazy when you were grieving.

I pumped you full of caffeine and adrenaline and called it ambition.

You didn't fail me—you were just trying to keep up.

I'm ready to go slower now.

Elena, 29 – a trauma survivor, began with:

Dear body,

I don't know how to feel you yet.

But I know I miss you.

Please don't give up on me while I learn how to come home.

Samira, 42 – a chronic people-pleaser, said:

My beautiful body,

I abandoned you to keep the peace.

I ignored your exhaustion to earn love.

But I'm ready to build a different kind of relationship—one where you come first.

Somatic Reflection Practice: Write Your Own Letter

You don't need to know what to say. You just need to start.

Try one of these prompts and write without editing:

- *Dear body, I'm sorry I...*
- *Dear body, thank you for...*
- *Dear body, I'm scared to feel you because...*
- *Dear body, I want to trust you, but...*

Don't worry about grammar or tone. This isn't for anyone else. This is for the part of you that's still waiting to be heard. You don't have to have the perfect relationship with your body. You just have to stop fighting it and start listening.

What you once called fatigue, dissociation, or panic might turn out to be your body's most honest prayer for peace.

Relearning the Language of the Body

The body speaks in sensations, not sentences. In recovery, part of healing is learning how to *listen again*. A tight chest might mean fear. Numbness might mean overwhelm. Butterflies might mean excitement or early anxiety. Learning this language helps you *respond* instead of react.

This section will explore:

- The nervous system's basic signals (fight, flight, freeze, fawn)
- How to track sensation without judgment
- Tools for increasing interoception (inner awareness)

Tone: Grounded, instructional

Practice: Somatic scanning + daily 2-minute body check-in

Touch, Movement, and Stillness: Returning Through the Senses

Trust isn't something the body regains through thinking. It comes back slowly, through lived experience, moments when the body realizes, *"This is safe. I'm allowed to be here."*

In addiction and trauma, the senses often get hijacked. We either feel *everything* too intensely or feel *nothing* at all. Recovery teaches us to come back to that middle ground, to rediscover the language of the senses, not as threats, but as invitations home.

Here's how that looked for a few people I've known on this journey.

Luis – The Washcloth Moment

For Luis, recovery didn't begin with a grand insight; it began with a hot washcloth.

He was anxious, overwhelmed, and riding the edge of a craving. His body was tight, his breathing shallow. He didn't know what he needed, but something inside whispered, *"Try warmth."*

So he soaked a cloth in hot water, pressed it to his face, and sat there breathing.

That was it. No words. No fixing. Just contact. Just presence.

Later, he told me, "That was the first time in months I didn't feel like I needed to escape my own skin."

Sometimes healing starts that small.

Tasha – The Kitchen Dance

Tasha was doing everything "right" in her program: attending meetings, staying connected, and staying sober. But she still felt trapped in her body, stiff and shut down. Joy felt unreachable.

One night, while cleaning up after dinner, she put on music, something old and familiar. Her hips started to move. Then her arms. Then her whole body was swaying, not because she had to, but because she *wanted* to.

"I hadn't moved like that in years," she told me. "I didn't even know I needed it until I started. And then I couldn't stop."

That night, Tasha said her body felt like a friend again.

Nadia – Learning to Be Still Without Shame

Nadia had always equated rest with laziness. She'd grown up believing she had to earn everything, including peace. Stillness made her anxious.

But early in sobriety, her body began refusing to push through. She started lying down in the afternoons, with no screen and no goal, just resting. At first, she hated it. Felt guilty. But one day, something shifted. She didn't force herself to get up. She just *let herself be.*

She said, "It was the first time in my life I rested without apology. And my body melted. It trusted me."

Stillness, once a punishment, became a sanctuary.

These Moments Matter

These stories aren't about breakthroughs. They're about *trust-building*.

A little heat. A little music. A moment on the couch without guilt.

They're proof that the body doesn't need to be "fixed"; it needs to be *felt*.

You don't have to master mindfulness or move like a dancer. You just have to let your body have what it's been missing.

Touch.

Movement.

Stillness.

Three quiet ways back to wholeness.

From Self-Management to Self-Relationship

For most of us, the early phases of recovery felt like trying to wrangle a wild animal, one we weren't sure we could trust.

We learned to manage our bodies.

We tracked cravings.

We white-knuckled through urges.

We made schedules to keep us from spiraling.

We controlled what we could so we wouldn't fall apart.

And that's okay. At one point, that structure saved us. It gave us shape and safety. However, over time, this kind of *management* can become a form of disconnection in itself.

Healing asks us to move beyond control. To go from managing the body to *relating* to it. To stop treating it like a project and start treating it like a partner.

Your Body Is Not a Problem to Solve

Real trust begins when we stop asking, *"What's wrong with me?"* and start asking, *"What do I need right now?"*

It's a subtle shift. But it's everything.

When your body tenses, it's not misbehaving; it's asking for support.

When your heart races, it's not sabotaging you; it's calling for regulation.

When you want to shut down, you're not failing; you're protecting.

Imagine waking up tomorrow and meeting your body like this:

"Good morning. I've got you today. Let's stay in touch."

That's relationship.

That's care.

That's what replaces the shame spiral with soft presence.

From Punishment to Partnership

We are so quick to punish ourselves:

- I should've eaten better.
- I shouldn't be this tired.
- I need to get it together.

But what if we met the body like we would a child or a dear friend?

Try saying:

- *"You seem overwhelmed. Let's slow down."*

- *"You've held a lot today. Let's rest."*
- *"You're feeling big things. I'm still here with you."*

These words are not fluff. They're regulation. They're healing.

Because every time you respond with compassion, you send your nervous system a new message:

"You're not alone anymore."

Try This: A Morning Body Dialogue

When you wake up tomorrow, place one hand on your heart or your belly and ask:

"What do you need today?"

You don't have to fix anything.

Just *listen.*

Maybe the answer is rest.

Maybe it's movement.

Maybe it's quiet.

Maybe it's a boundary.

Maybe it's a meal.

And whatever it is, whisper back, *"I've got you."*

That's it. That's the new relationship. One that's built on consent, kindness, and care.

You're not here to conquer your body.

You're here to return to it.

You're not here to master sobriety through control.

You're here to embody recovery through connection.

And your body?

It's not resisting you.

It's been *waiting for you.*

Chapter Summary

In this chapter, we explored the slow, sacred process of rebuilding trust with the body after trauma and addiction. We reframed symptoms like fatigue, tension, and anxiety as *messages*, not failures. We listened to stories of reconnection through warmth, movement, and stillness. And we shifted from controlling the body to relating to it with compassion, curiosity, and care.

This isn't about getting it perfect. It's about showing up in small, consistent ways that say:

"I'm with you now. We're doing this together."

The body you once feared is becoming the home you're learning to live in again.

Now that you've started building a relationship with your body, it's time to deepen your toolkit. In the next chapter, we'll walk through grounded, body-based practices that help regulate the nervous system, prevent relapse, and support long-term recovery.

This isn't about routines; it's about *rituals of safety.* Let's explore what healing *looks like in motion.*

21

PRACTICAL TECHNIQUES FOR HEALING AND RECOVERY

THE POWER OF RITUAL: MAKING HEALING TANGIBLE

In somatic therapy, we learn that the nervous system doesn't speak in logic or language; it speaks in rhythm, repetition, and felt experience. That's why ritual becomes so essential in recovery. Not for its mystique but for its predictability. It offers something the traumatized body rarely had: safety through consistency.

Long before therapy, ritual was the language of healing in cultures around the world—through dance, drumming, water, breath, and prayer. These weren't luxuries. They were medicine. They helped regulate the body, express emotion, and restore coherence.

Ritual is somatic. It tells the body: *you are held, you are here, you are no longer alone.*

Ritual vs. Routine A routine is for productivity. A ritual is for presence. It doesn't matter what the act is—what matters is how it's done. Lighting a candle. Saying a phrase. Putting lotion on your hands slowly. Drinking tea with intention. These are not habits—they're messages of safety written in sensation.

When we ritualize small acts with care and rhythm, we reclaim our right to exist safely in our body. We begin to repair the ruptures of trauma, not with logic, but with repetition. With reverence.

Recovery Rituals in Real Life

- Alma places both hands over her heart each morning and whispers, "We've got this today."
- DeShawn takes five deep breaths before walking into any room where he might feel pressure or fear.
- Rina ends her day by massaging her hands and saying, "Thank you for what you carried."
- Cameron dips his fingers in water before bed, saying, "Let it be cleansed."

These are not acts of perfection. They are nervous system recalibrations. They are how the body learns: *This time, we're doing it differently.*

Breath as a Somatic Anchor

Breath is the body's built-in rhythm keeper. In trauma and addiction, that rhythm gets distorted—shortened, held, forgotten. Even in recovery, we often don't know how to breathe with our whole body. We're either rushing forward or bracing for impact.

The breath doesn't fix anything. It *roots* us. It keeps us here when we want to run or numb.

Pendulum Breath: A Nervous System Swing This breath pattern mimics the soothing motion of rocking—an ancient form of regulation. It helps downshift anxiety, thaw freeze, and bring the body back into rhythm.

Try This:

1. Sit or lie down. Rest your hands on your chest and belly.
2. Inhale through your nose for 4 counts.
3. Pause for 2 counts—rest, don't hold.
4. Exhale through your mouth for 4 counts.

5. Pause again for 2 counts.

Repeat for 3–5 minutes. Let the rhythm hold you like a gentle swing. Notice how your body shifts: does your jaw soften? Do your shoulders drop? Do tears come? Let the pendulum guide you back.

When to Use It:

- When you feel a craving, trigger, or emotional spike
- Before entering a stressful space
- To recover after a shame spiral
- As a daily practice for steadying your system

You don't need to force calm. You just need to stay in the swing.

NEW PRACTICE: THE 5-4-3-2-1 NATURE RESET

A Somatic Ritual for Overwhelm, Anxiety, or Disconnection

This outdoor-based practice rewires the body's sense of safety through direct engagement with the natural world. It's a grounding technique adapted for recovery that reconnects you with your senses in real time.

How to Do It:

1. Go outside—anywhere. A park. A yard. A quiet sidewalk.
2. Take one slow breath.
3. Identify:
    - **5 things you see** (a tree, a flower, clouds, sidewalk texture)
    - **4 things you can touch** (bark, stone, your clothing, a leaf)
    - **3 things you hear** (wind, birds, traffic)
    - **2 things you smell** (air, dirt, grass)
    - **1 thing you taste** (or simply feel your tongue or breath)
4. Place your hand on your chest and say: *"I am here. I am in the world. I am allowed to stay."*

Why It Works: This practice activates orienting, a somatic tool that anchors the nervous system in the present moment. Nature provides multisensory input that helps co-regulate without the need for screens or stimulation.

Use it:

- When emotions are too big to name
- When inside feels suffocating
- As a transition between chaos and calm

This is not a distraction. It's return. It's presence. It's embodied hope.

The techniques in this chapter are not meant to be mastered all at once. Choose one. Practice slowly. Let your nervous system build trust with the tools.

Somatic recovery isn't about performing better; it's about learning to stay. With your body. With your breath. With your truth.

Creating a Daily Somatic Practice (That You'll Actually Use)

Consistency without perfection—your nervous system's rhythm for healing

You don't need a perfect routine. You don't need a 90-minute practice with incense, mantras, or a yoga mat. You just need a rhythm, a way to return to your body *on purpose* every day. A somatic practice is not about "doing it right." It's about building a relationship with your nervous system, one that says:

"I will keep showing up for you, even when it's hard."

WHY ROUTINE MATTERS FOR THE NERVOUS SYSTEM

Our nervous systems crave predictability, especially after trauma, chaos, or addiction. When we return to the same supportive practices, even in small doses, we create neural safety. We signal to the body:

"This is familiar. This is okay. We've been here before."

That familiarity builds capacity, the ability to feel more, stay longer, and regulate more easily when challenges arise. This is why daily somatic rituals, even the smallest ones, are more powerful than occasional, large practices. It's not about how long. It's about how often.

What Makes a Somatic Practice "Work"?

It's not complexity.

It's *connection*.

A sustainable somatic practice is one that:

- Honors your current capacity
- Is doable on your worst days
- Involves sensation, breath, movement, or stillness
- Leaves you feeling more present, not more judged

Morning Practice: Start with Presence (5–10 minutes)

Try:

- 1 minute of hand-on-heart breath
- Name one sensation in your body
- Say a somatic mantra: *"I'm here. I'm listening."*
- Gentle movement: sway, stretch, shake
- One intention: *"What do I need to stay steady today?"*

Evening Practice: Come Home to Yourself (5–10 minutes)

Try:

- Wash your hands or face slowly (temperature + texture grounding)
- Reflect: *What did my body carry today?*
- Journaling or simply sitting in silence
- Touch: lotion on hands, hand to chest, warmth
- Whisper: *"Thank you for staying."*

Don't Force It—Flex It

You don't need the same practice every day. You need the same message:

"I'm here. I care. I'm not abandoning you."

Some days that might mean:

- One breath
- A stretch before bed
- Putting your hand on your belly while stuck in traffic

These micro-moments matter. They teach your body:

"Relapse isn't the only option. Disconnection isn't the only answer. I have another way now."

Build Your Own Somatic Rhythm (Simple Menu)

Pick 1 from each category to create your custom 5–10 min practice:

- **Breath**: Pendulum breath, sighing, belly breathing
- **Touch**: Hand to chest, wrapping hold, textured object
- **Movement**: Sway, shake, stretch, rock
- **Stillness**: Eyes closed, orienting gaze, body scan
- **Words**: Somatic mantra, prayer, simple "thank you"

Optional journal prompt: *"What part of me needed this today?"*

You Don't Need More Discipline—You Need More Care

This is not about compliance.

This is not about checking boxes.

This is about *devotion to your own aliveness.*

When you build a daily somatic rhythm, even the smallest one, you're building:

- A nervous system that can hold more without numbing
- A body that trusts it will be listened to
- A life that no longer runs from itself

You don't need to wait until you feel healed to start.

You don't need to do it perfectly every day.

You just need to return.

Again and again.

This is how we recover.

This is how we come home.

Chapter Summary

In this chapter, we redefined what real healing looks like: not dramatic breakthroughs or spiritual fireworks but consistent return. You learned that somatic practices don't need to be fancy or long; they just need to be honest. A hand on the chest. A breath that doesn't leave you. A movement that helps you stay.

You explored the power of ritual, breath, grounding, emotional processing, affirmation, and daily rhythm. Each practice is an invitation to come home to the body, to the moment, and to your sober self. You don't have to do it all. You just have to keep coming back.

As we step into this next chapter, we leave behind "early sobriety" as a phase and begin to explore recovery as a *way of life*. This is where the real transformation begins.

This is where you don't just survive without substances.

You learn to live fully inside your skin.

This chapter is about what happens when somatic healing becomes not just a set of tools, but a deep, living relationship with your body, your story, and your soul.

22

LONG-TERM RECOVERY AND THE EMBODIED SELF

Long-term recovery is not the absence of cravings; it's the presence of wholeness. It's when sobriety stops being a fight and starts becoming a rhythm. A returning. A reclaiming.

For many of us, early recovery is marked by urgency, a desperate attempt to stabilize and not fall apart. It's raw, fragile, and exhausting. But with time, something shifts. Recovery becomes less about holding on and more about coming home. The body, once a battleground, becomes a guide. The nervous system, once trapped in cycles of survival, begins to trust. This is the essence of long-term sobriety: the evolution from self-control to self-connection.

This chapter is not just about maintaining sobriety; it's about deepening into it. It's about embodiment, not as a concept, but as a lived reality. As we integrate the somatic path we've walked together, we'll explore what long-term healing actually *feels* like, in the body, in the breath, and in the quiet truths that begin to surface when we are no longer just surviving.

Let's explore this through four deep sections:

THE MOMENT IT CHANGED

For many people, long-term recovery arrives without fanfare. There's no thunderclap, no parade, just a quiet moment of realization. It might be the first time you laughed without guilt. Or sat through discomfort without fleeing. Or trusted yourself with a secret you used to run from.

These moments might arise in the most ordinary situations: a silent morning walk where you notice birdsong, a peaceful evening alone where loneliness doesn't echo as loudly or the realization that you've gone weeks without needing to numb or escape. These moments aren't flashy, but they are *foundational*. They signal that your body has started to trust safety again.

Example: M., a woman in recovery, shares her turning point: "I used to avoid mirrors. One day, I didn't. I smiled. Not because I liked what I saw, but because I *saw* myself, and I didn't turn away. That's when I knew I wasn't just sober. I was healing."

Long-term recovery is a new way of relating to yourself. It's what happens when you no longer have to fear who you are in silence. It is the softening of hypervigilance, the surrendering of control, and the discovery that life can unfold *with* you, not against you.

WRITING TO THE BODY THAT STAYED

Long-term recovery is marked by a return to the body, not as something to fix but something to befriend. One of the most powerful somatic practices in sustained healing is writing a letter to your body. This ritual of recognition and gratitude acknowledges the deep intelligence of the body that never abandoned you, even when you abandoned it.

"Dear body, thank you. For staying. For enduring. For remembering how to breathe when I forgot. For holding pain I couldn't name. I blamed you when

you were trying to protect me. I judged you when you were doing your best to survive. Now I know better."

These letters often express grief, for the years of pushing through, of ignoring fatigue, of denying hunger and touch. They also reveal profound joy: the return of appetite, sleep, tears, laughter, and sexual desire, as well as movement. Everything that addiction tried to numb.

Let's hear from a few fictionalized composite voices:

- **Thomas**, 52, wrote to his hands, once used to grip bottles, now used to hold his granddaughter.
- **Jada**, 29, penned a letter to her hips, which she'd spent years hating, now honoring the way they carried her through trauma and into dance.
- **River**, nonbinary and in their mid-30s, wrote to their chest, acknowledging years of disconnection and finally celebrating how it now rises and falls with breath, with pride.

Writing to the body becomes an act of embodiment. It says: *"I am here now." "I choose to stay."*

TOUCH, MOVEMENT, AND STILLNESS: RETURNING THROUGH THE SENSES

Trust is not rebuilt in the mind; it's rebuilt in the body. The nervous system, conditioned for years to anticipate chaos, learns safety through repetition, gentleness, and sensory truth. In long-term recovery, this means engaging the body not for productivity or appearance but for presence.

Touch, movement, and stillness become your companions. Each holds a specific medicine:

- **Touch** grounds you in contact. A palm on your heart. A warm bath. A weighted blanket. A textured object that helps you feel tethered.

- **Movement** reminds you that you are not stuck. Gentle rocking, slow walking, yoga, or swaying while brushing your teeth all invite fluidity where rigidity once ruled.
- **Stillness** is perhaps the most radical act—allowing the body to settle without fleeing into activity or distraction. It's in these pauses that integration occurs.

These acts of sensory return teach your nervous system: "It's safe now. You can be here." Over time, these practices become as natural as breathing. They're not tricks or hacks; they're ancient languages the body understands.

From Self-Management to Self-Relationship

In the beginning, sobriety often demands structure: managing cravings, keeping a routine, and attending meetings. This structure provides safety. But as recovery matures, something deeper becomes possible: the shift from management to relationship.

In long-term recovery, you begin to:

- Ask *why* your body reacts, not just how to stop it
- Offer compassion instead of criticism
- Recognize that urges are messengers, not enemies

This is what self-relationship looks like: you sit with discomfort instead of fleeing it. You learn your rhythms and honor your capacity. You no longer punish the body; you partner with it.

This doesn't mean life gets easier—it means you get more resourced to meet it. You begin to live with your body, not against it. You know how to pause. How to check in. How to repair. How to forgive. And maybe most importantly, how to *stay*.

In this place, long-term recovery reveals itself not as a rigid state but as a relational one. You are constantly evolving, and so is your healing. And that's okay.

Chapter Summary

Long-term recovery is not a plateau; it's an expansion. A return to the full range of human experience, with the body as your guide and companion. It's the gentle shift from surviving to inhabiting. From control to collaboration. From fixing to befriending.

You don't arrive at healing; it unfolds. It deepens each time you choose to stay present. It expands each time you trust your body's signals. It softens each time you treat yourself with the tenderness you once reserved for others.

As we move into the final chapter, we'll explore what it means to embody sobriety not just as a practice but as a way of living. A way of *being* that honors the depth of everything you've walked through and the beauty of everything yet to come.

23

A NEW KIND OF SOBRIETY

BEYOND ABSTINENCE—THE EMBODIED AWAKENING

Sobriety isn't the end of something; it's the beginning of everything. It's not just putting down the drink; it's picking up your life with both hands. For many, early recovery is a sprint through shame, withdrawals, and white-knuckled days. But long-term sobriety, sustained, somatic, and sacred, is about learning to live inside your body again. It's about finding safety in your skin and trust in your breath.

Mark knew the wreckage well. A father of three, he drank through birthdays, missed holidays, and once forgot to pick up his youngest son from school. His wife left after his third DUI. His children stopped answering his calls. When he finally got sober at 46, his liver was failing, and so was his hope. What AA started, somatic work sustained. Mark began to feel his way back to life. He realized his jaw clenched when he felt unheard. That his stomach twisted in shame before he ever reached for a drink. That his hands trembled not because he was weak but because his body was begging for safety.

The Quiet Miracle of Everyday Presence

Five years into recovery, Mark's life didn't look like a redemption movie. He had a modest apartment, a quiet job repairing HVAC systems, and a court-ordered co-parenting plan. But something had shifted in him. When his teenage son finally agreed to spend the weekend, Mark didn't panic or over-plan. He embodied his recovery in every moment.

He knelt to tie his son's shoelace and noticed the ache in his knees. He laughed without needing to perform. He cooked dinner slowly, savoring the scent of garlic, letting himself feel the joy of feeding someone he loved. And when the weekend ended, he didn't numb the grief. He let the tears come. Because his nervous system could finally hold the weight of feeling without collapsing.

This is the miracle of embodied sobriety. Not perfection, but presence. Not control, but connection. Mark's healing wasn't flashy; it was quiet, cellular, and real. A nervous system once on fire with fear now pulsed with the slow, steady rhythm of re-engagement.

The Spiral Path—Staying, Returning, Deepening

Healing doesn't move in straight lines. It spirals. Triggers return. Grief returns. The body remembers. But now, we remember, too. We remember how to pause. How to breathe. How to come home.

Mark still gets overwhelmed at work, in parenting, and in grief. But now he notices it. His chest tightens. His shoulders rise. And instead of reaching for relief in a bottle, he reaches for regulation: a walk, a phone call, and a few deep exhales in the car before walking into a hard moment.

This is how recovery lives in the body: not as a performance of perfection but as a practiced return to safety. It's how Mark parents now, not with guilt for the years he lost, but with presence for the moments he has. Sobriety, for him, became a way of reparenting himself and showing his son that strength isn't about not falling; it's about knowing how to rise.

A LEGACY WRITTEN IN THE BODY

Mark's story is one of rupture and repair. Of losing everything, then finding himself. Not all at once, but breath by breath, boundary by boundary. His story is echoed in countless others: people who thought they were too far gone, only to discover that healing was not about becoming someone new; it was about remembering who they were before the pain.

This new kind of sobriety is rooted in presence, not performance. It's about learning to feel again through the awkwardness, the tenderness, the joy, and even the rage. It's about parenting with a regulated heart. Partnering without shame. Living in rhythm with your breath instead of bracing against it.

You won't always get it right. That's not the point. The point is you stay. You soften. You return.

This is the sobriety that lasts, the one no one can take from you because it lives in your bones. In your choices. In the way you show up.

You don't have to become someone else to deserve it. You just have to keep becoming yourself.

This is the new kind of sobriety. And you're already living it.

Conclusion: The Steps Were in You All Along

This book began as an invitation to see recovery not just as abstinence but as a return. A return to your breath, your skin, your pulse. A return to the parts of yourself that addiction tried to exile, that trauma taught you to silence. But what unfolded across these chapters wasn't just a theory or a method. It was a living experience, a somatic retelling of the 12 Steps, not only as ideas but as experiences you carry in the tissue of your being.

For so long, many of us walked through recovery, trying to think our way through pain, trying to reason with cravings, trying to muscle our way through old wounds. But the body does not speak in thoughts. It speaks in sensation. Tightness, restlessness, collapse. Heat in the cheeks. Numbness in the hands. These were the first signals that something in us was calling out, not to be fixed but to be felt. To be heard.

In this book, you learned how Step One is more than admission. It's the moment your body could finally stop pretending it was fine. It's the sigh, the slouch, the tears you didn't plan. You learned that Step Four wasn't just a moral inventory; it was a somatic excavation. The turning inward, the trembling honesty, the shaking hands that still chose to write it down. Step Nine became less about external reconciliation and more about internal repair. Not everyone gets to hear "I'm sorry." But your nervous system can.

Each step along the way, you didn't just think; you felt. And in feeling, you healed.

This way of recovery is slow. It's tender. It doesn't shout. It listens. It asks questions like, "What do I need right now?" instead of "What's wrong with me?" It pauses instead of punishes. It doesn't demand perfection; it invites presence. You learned that regulation is not a performance. It is a practice. A whisper back to the body that says, "I'm here. I'm staying."

You built boundaries not from fear but from self-respect. You began to see your triggers not as shameful setbacks but as information, as maps showing you where your nervous system still longs for care. You stopped chasing a fantasy version of healing and began living it, moment by moment, in the real textures of your life, in your morning breath, in your palms against warm water, in the stillness before sleep.

And as you did, the 12 Steps transformed. They stopped being commandments carved in stone and started becoming living rhythms within you:

- Admitting powerlessness not as defeat but as surrender into support.

- Believing in a power greater than yourself, not just outside you, but within your breath, your bones, your belly.
- Turning over your will, not in fear, but in faith that the body knows what healing looks like.
- Making amends, not just with others, but with the exiled parts of yourself.

You've come to understand that your nervous system is not your enemy. It's your oldest companion. It learned to survive in remarkable ways. And now, in recovery, it is learning to trust again. With every pause, every breath, every time you chose to feel instead of flee, you laid down new pathways. Not overnight. But over time. That is what healing asks for.

If you've made it to this point, I want you to stop for a moment. Place a hand on your chest. Notice that you are still here.

That matters. That means something.

You are not broken. You are brave. You are learning to live in your body again—and that is no small thing. That is revolutionary.

As you continue on this path, remember: The Steps are not behind you now. They are within you. They live in how you breathe when you're scared, how you soften when you're safe, and how you stay when it would be easier to run. They are written not just in your journal or on your chip but in the very tissues of your being.

This book may be coming to an end, but your journey is not. Let this be a threshold, not a finish line. Let it be a reminder that sobriety is not just the absence of a substance; it's the presence of self. It's not just surviving without a drink. It's learning to dance with life again, with all of it: the pain, the pleasure, the pauses, the pulse.

May your body always be your guide. May your breath always bring you home. And may you never forget:

You didn't just follow the Steps. You became them.

With all my heart,

M. Sallie

A Letter to You, the Reader

Dear Friend,

If you're reading this, you made it to the end.

But more importantly, you stayed.

Maybe you stayed sober today.

Maybe you came back after a relapse.

Maybe you're just now realizing it's time to try something different.

Whatever brought you here, I want you to know this:

You are not broken.

You are not too far gone.

You are not alone.

I didn't write this book as an expert. I wrote it as someone who has sat where you may be sitting. I've known the ache of regret. I've felt the silent collapse inside my chest. I've stared at the ceiling, wondering if I could really do this again. I've walked into meetings feeling raw and unsure, and walked out just a little more whole.

But I also know what it feels like to come back into my body.

To take a breath and know it's mine.

To look in the mirror and not look away.

To feel the peace of choosing presence over punishment, even for just a moment.

This journey is not about perfection.

It's about returning.

Again and again and again, until that return becomes your rhythm.

You don't need to be more disciplined.

You don't need to be more spiritual.

You just need to be willing to stay a little longer with yourself than you used to.

This book is a collection of what helped me stay.

It's a map, written in the language of the body, in the hope that you, too, might find your way back, not just to sobriety, but to *you*.

To the you who is soft and brave.

To the you who is tired and still trying.

To the you who wants to feel safe in your own skin.

To the you who is learning that peace is not earned—it's remembered.

If no one has told you this today:

I'm proud of you. I really am.

For reading. For pausing. For not giving up.

For letting yourself imagine a life beyond surviving.

Keep choosing yourself.

Keep coming home.

I'll be right here with you; in every breath, every pause, every sacred return.

With love and deep respect,

M. Sallie

GLOSSARY OF SOMATIC AND RECOVERY TERMS

Below is a comprehensive glossary of terms related to somatic therapy and recovery. The terms encompass key concepts, practices, and approaches relevant to somatic therapy, trauma, addiction recovery, and related practices discussed in the book.

- **Addiction**: A condition often characterized as a disease of the mind, body, and spirit, where substances or behaviors are used to cope with overwhelming pain, trauma, or emotional dysregulation. In the somatic context, addiction is viewed as a body-based survival strategy to manage an overwhelmed nervous system.
- **Alexander Technique**: A somatic practice that focuses on improving posture and movement efficiency through conscious awareness of bodily habits. In recovery, it supports reconnection to the body, particularly for those healing from chronic tension or dissociation.
- **Anchor Points**: A grounding technique where an individual presses their feet into the floor, thighs into a chair, or hands against thighs to activate proprioception, helping to interrupt spiraling thoughts or dissociation and bring awareness back to the present.

- **Bioenergetic Analysis**: A somatic therapy developed by Alexander Lowen that combines physical exercises, breathwork, and body awareness to release emotional blocks held in the body. In recovery, it aids in reconnecting with suppressed feelings and restoring emotional expression.
- **Body-Based Healing**: Healing approaches that prioritize the body's role in processing trauma and supporting recovery. These include practices like Somatic Experiencing, trauma-sensitive yoga, and breathwork, which aim to restore safety and regulation in the nervous system.
- **Body Scan**: A somatic practice involving a slow, mindful check-in with different parts of the body to notice sensations, tension, or discomfort. It helps increase interoception and fosters a gentle reconnection with the body.
- **Breathwork**: Guided breathing techniques used to regulate emotions, increase interoception, and calm the nervous system. In recovery, breathwork serves as a tool for grounding, managing cravings, and re-establishing a connection with the body.
- **Co-Regulation**: The process by which one person's nervous system helps regulate another's through shared presence, touch, or emotional attunement. In somatic therapy, practices like the Wrapping Hold mimic co-regulation to promote safety and calm.
- **Craniosacral Therapy**: A gentle, hands-on somatic technique that supports the body's natural rhythms and releases tension in the nervous system. In recovery, it helps with emotional shutdown, chronic fatigue, or deep stress states.
- **Dissociation**: A state where an individual feels disconnected from their body, emotions, or surroundings, often as a protective response to trauma or overwhelm. Somatic therapy aims to gently reconnect individuals to their bodily sensations to reduce dissociation.
- **Dorsal Vagal Collapse (Shutdown/Freeze)**: A state of the nervous system associated with the dorsal vagal branch of the parasympathetic nervous system, characterized by numbness,

fog, or emotional withdrawal. It's a survival response to overwhelming stress or trauma.
- **Embodied Affirmations (Somatic Mantras)**: Phrases paired with physical gestures, breath, or touch to speak directly to the nervous system, fostering safety and self-compassion. Unlike traditional affirmations, they are designed to feel believable and resonate with the body's current capacity.
- **Embodied Resilience**: The ability to feel, adapt, and respond to life's challenges without needing to shut down or escape, built through somatic practices like movement, breathwork, and grounding. It supports long-term recovery by fostering presence and emotional capacity.
- **Emotional Capacity**: The ability to experience and process emotions without becoming overwhelmed or needing to numb them. Somatic therapy builds this capacity through practices like titration and pendulation, allowing individuals to stay present with feelings.
- **Fawn Response**: A trauma response where an individual seeks to appease or please others to avoid harm or conflict, often at the expense of their own needs. In recovery, somatic practices help individuals recognize and shift this pattern to build self-respect and boundaries.
- **Feldenkrais Method**: A somatic approach using slow, gentle movements and awareness to retrain the nervous system and improve physical and emotional functioning. In recovery, it supports self-awareness, reduces tension, and fosters calm presence.
- **Fight-or-Flight Response**: A survival response of the sympathetic nervous system characterized by heightened arousal, such as a racing heart, quick breathing, or tense muscles, preparing the body to confront or flee from danger. Chronic activation can contribute to anxiety and addiction.
- **Grounding**: Somatic techniques that reconnect an individual to the present moment through sensory engagement with the body or environment. Examples include Anchor Points, Orienting Through the Eyes, and

Touch + Temperature Reset, used to manage cravings or dysregulation.
- **Hakomi Method**: A somatic therapy developed by Ron Kurtz that uses mindfulness and body awareness to uncover unconscious beliefs stored in posture, breath, and sensation. In recovery, it helps transform beliefs like "I'm not safe" that drive addiction.
- **Interoception**: The ability to sense and interpret internal bodily signals, such as heartbeat, breath, or muscle tension. In recovery, developing interoception helps individuals notice triggers and respond to their body's needs without numbing.
- **Muscular Armoring**: A concept introduced by Wilhelm Reich, referring to chronic muscle tension or rigidity developed as a protective response to trauma or emotional repression. Somatic therapy works to release this armoring to restore ease and emotional flow.
- **Nervous System Dysregulation**: A state where the nervous system is stuck in survival modes (fight, flight, freeze, or fawn), leading to symptoms like anxiety, numbness, or emotional overwhelm. Somatic therapy aims to restore regulation and balance.
- **Orientation**: A somatic practice of locating oneself in time and space, often through visual or sensory engagement with the environment, to reduce dissociation and restore a sense of presence. Example: naming five neutral or pleasant objects in the surroundings.
- **Pendulation**: A somatic technique that involves gently shifting attention between stressful and calming sensations to process trauma without overwhelm. It helps the nervous system move between activation and safety, fostering regulation.
- **Pendulum Breath**: A rhythmic breathing practice (inhale-pause-exhale-pause) that mimics natural movement to regulate emotional swings and return the nervous system to a grounded state. It's particularly effective for dorsal vagal or sympathetic states.

- **Proprioception**: The body's sense of its position and movement in space, activated through grounding techniques like pressing feet into the floor. It helps interrupt dissociation and anchors the body in the present.
- **Regulation**: The ability to notice and manage nervous system arousal (e.g., fight, flight, freeze) and return to a state of calm and presence. Somatic therapy teaches regulation through breath, movement, and grounding to support sobriety.
- **Reiki**: A Japanese energy healing technique involving light touch or hovering to channel universal life energy, promoting relaxation and emotional regulation. In recovery, it complements somatic practices by easing withdrawal symptoms and fostering mind-body connection.
- **Resourcing**: A somatic technique where individuals recall a supportive memory, image, or sensation to create a sense of safety and calm. It helps the nervous system shift from distress to a regulated state.
- **Ritual**: Intentional, embodied practices that provide predictability and sensory grounding to the nervous system, such as hand-on-heart breathing or slow hand washing. In recovery, rituals foster safety and connection, distinct from routines which focus on efficiency.
- **Somatic Experiencing (SE)**: A body-based therapy developed by Peter Levine that helps release trauma stored in the nervous system by tracking sensations and completing survival responses. In recovery, it reduces anxiety, triggers, and relapse risk.
- **Somatic Mantra**: See *Embodied Affirmations*.
- **Somatic Memories**: Sensations or tensions held in the body as a result of unprocessed trauma, such as tightness in the chest or knots in muscles. Somatic therapy works to gently release these memories to restore ease.
- **Somatic Readiness**: The state of having enough internal safety and nervous system regulation to engage in recovery work, such as the 12 Steps, without becoming overwhelmed.

It involves practices like grounding and breathwork to build stability.
- **Somatic Scanning**: A practice of mindfully observing bodily sensations to increase awareness and connection. It's used to identify areas of tension or discomfort and support nervous system regulation.
- **Somatic Therapy**: A therapeutic approach that emphasizes the body's role in healing trauma and addiction by addressing nervous system dysregulation and stored sensations. It includes methods like Somatic Experiencing, breathwork, and trauma-sensitive yoga.
- **Sympathetic Arousal**: A state of the nervous system characterized by heightened alertness, such as rapid heartbeat or tense muscles, associated with fight-or-flight responses. Somatic practices help down-regulate this state to restore calm.
- **Tension & Trauma Releasing Exercises (TRE)**: A somatic method developed by David Berceli that uses specific exercises to induce natural tremors, releasing deep tension and trauma. In recovery, it helps express emotions non-verbally.
- **Titration**: A somatic technique of processing trauma in small, manageable doses to avoid overwhelm, allowing the nervous system to gradually release stored energy and build resilience.
- **Trauma**: The lasting impact of overwhelming experiences on the nervous system, stored as physical sensations or dysregulation, not just the event itself. In recovery, somatic therapy addresses trauma's bodily effects to support healing.
- **Trauma-Sensitive Yoga**: A form of yoga adapted for trauma survivors, focusing on gentle movement, choice, and body awareness rather than performance. In recovery, it helps manage anxiety and rebuild physical trust.
- **Window of Tolerance**: The range of nervous system arousal where an individual can stay present, think clearly, and make conscious choices. Somatic practices help expand this window to manage triggers and emotions in recovery.

REFERENCES

Alm, B. (2018). The neuroscience of craving: Understanding addiction through brain imaging. *Neuroscience & Biobehavioral Reviews, 96*, 130–143. https://doi.org/10.1016/j.neubiorev.2018.10.016

American Psychiatric Association. (2013). *Diagnostic and statistical manual of mental disorders* (5th ed.). American Psychiatric Publishing.

Anda, R. F., Butchart, A., Felitti, V. J., & Brown, D. W. (2010). Building a framework for global surveillance of the public health implications of adverse childhood experiences. *American Journal of Preventive Medicine, 39*(1), 93–98. https://doi.org/10.1016/j.amepre.2010.03.015

Barton, J., & Rogerson, M. (2017). The importance of greenspace for mental health. *BJPsych International, 14*(4), 79–81. https://doi.org/10.1192/s2056474000002054

Beck, J. M., & Parra, L. L. (2018). Somatic integration of 12-Step: A pilot study. *Alcoholism Treatment Quarterly, 36*(4), 349–365. https://doi.org/10.1080/07347324.2018.1503106

Benson, H., & Stark, M. (1985). Mind/body medicine: A unified model for common ailments. *Archives of Internal Medicine, 145*(8), 1447–1452. https://doi.org/10.1001/archinte.145.8.1447

Bowen, S., Chawla, N., & Marlatt, G. A. (2014). *Mindfulness-based relapse prevention for addictive behaviors: A clinician's guide.* Guilford Press.

Craig, A. D. (2003). Interoception: The sense of the physiological condition of the body. *Current Opinion in Neurobiology, 13*(4), 500–505. https://doi.org/10.1016/S0959-4388(03)00090-4

Creswell, J. D. (2017). Mindfulness interventions. *Annual Review of Psychology, 68*, 491–516. https://doi.org/10.1146/annurev-psych-042716-051139

De Leon, G. (2015). The role of recovery models in substance abuse treatment. *Journal of Psychoactive Drugs, 47*(3), 213–221. https://doi.org/10.1080/02791072.2015.1052623

Dutra, L., Stathopoulou, G., Basden, S. L., Leyro, T. M., Powers, M. B., & Otto, M. W. (2008). A meta-analytic review of psychosocial interventions for substance use disorders. *American Journal of Psychiatry, 165*(2), 179–187. https://doi.org/10.1176/appi.ajp.2007.06111851

Emerson, D., Hopper, E., & van der Kolk, B. A. (2009). *Trauma-sensitive yoga in therapy: Bringing the body into treatment.* W. W. Norton.

Felitti, V. J., Anda, R. F., Nordenberg, D., Williamson, D. F., Spitz, A. M., Edwards, V., Koss, M. P., & Marks, J. S. (1998). Relationship of childhood abuse and household dysfunction to many of the leading causes of death in adults: The Adverse Childhood Experiences (ACE) Study. *American Journal of Preventive Medicine, 14*(4), 245–258. https://doi.org/10.1016/S0749-3797(98)00017-8

Feldenkrais, M. (1977). *Awareness through movement: Easy-to-do health exercises to improve your posture, vision, mood, and quality of life.* Harper & Row.

Gilligan, S. G. (2015). *The neuroscience of psychotherapy: Healing the social brain* (2nd ed.). W. W. Norton.

Gray, J. R., & Meyer, T. (2017). Polyvagal-informed practices for addiction recovery. *Journal of Addiction Research & Therapy, 8*(4), 1000e123. https://doi.org/10.4172/2155-6105.1000e123

Gannon, R., & Furey, S. (2016). Tension & Trauma Releasing Exercises (TRE) and addiction: A case series. *Journal of Bodywork & Movement Therapies, 20*(3), 528–535. https://doi.org/10.1016/j.jbmt.2016.03.003

Garland, E. L., Froeliger, B., & Howard, M. O. (2019). Restructuring reward mechanisms in the treatment of addiction: A pilot fMRI study of mindfulness-oriented recovery enhancement for opioid dependence. *NeuroImage: Clinical, 24,* 102058. https://doi.org/10.1016/j.nicl.2019.102058

Gray, J. R. (2018). The polyvagal theory: A practitioner's guide. *Clinical Social Work Journal, 46*(1), 1–12. https://doi.org/10.1007/s10615-017-0631-9

Hayes, S. C., Luoma, J. B., Bond, F. W., Masuda, A., & Lillis, J. (2006). Acceptance and commitment therapy: Model, processes and outcomes. *Behaviour Research and Therapy, 44*(1), 1–25. https://doi.org/10.1016/j.brat.2005.06.006

Hölzel, B. K., Lazar, S. W., Gard, T., Schuman-Olivier, Z., Vago, D. R., & Ott, U. (2011). How does mindfulness meditation work? Proposing mechanisms of action from a conceptual and neural perspective. *Perspectives on Psychological Science, 6*(6), 537–559. https://doi.org/10.1177/1745691611419671

Kabat-Zinn, J. (1990). *Full catastrophe living: Using the wisdom of your body and mind to face stress, pain, and illness.* Delacorte.

Kaplan, R., & Kaplan, S. (1989). *The experience of nature: A psychological perspective.* Cambridge University Press.

Kilpatrick, D. G., Resnick, H. S., Acierno, R., Saunders, B. E., Best, C. L., & Schnurr, P. P. (2013). Posttraumatic stress disorder associated with exposure to the 2004 Florida hurricanes. *Journal of Consulting and Clinical Psychology, 81*(3), 299–310. https://doi.org/10.1037/a0032465

Kuhfuß, M., Vermetten, E., & Schauer, M. (2021). Somatic Experiencing – effectiveness and key factors of a body-oriented trauma therapy: A scoping literature review. *European Journal of Psychotraumatology, 12*(1), 1866607. https://doi.org/10.1080/20008198.2020.1866607

Leitch, L. (2007). *Waves of recovery: Somatic Experiencing in addiction.* Unpublished doctoral dissertation, California Institute of Integral Studies.

Lee, C. W., Scragg, P., & Lambert, S. (2020). EMDR for co-occurring PTSD and substance use disorders: A meta-analysis. *Journal of Anxiety Disorders, 75,* 102273. https://doi.org/10.1016/j.janxdis.2020.102273

Levine, P. A. (1997). *Waking the tiger: Healing trauma – The innate capacity to transform overwhelming experiences.* North Atlantic Books.

Logan, D. E., & King, T. S. (2001). Self-harm behaviors in a community sample of adolescents: Facilitators and inhibitors. *Suicide and Life-Threatening Behavior, 31*(3), 256–268. https://doi.org/10.1521/suli.31.3.256.24206

Lowen, A. (1975). *Bioenergetics: The revolutionary therapy that uses the language of the body to heal the problems of the mind.* Coward, McCann & Geoghegan.

Mehling, W. E., Price, C., Daubenmier, J., Acree, M., Bartmess, E., & Stewart, A. (2012). The Multidimensional Assessment of Interoceptive Awareness (MAIA). *PLoS ONE, 7*(11), e48230. https://doi.org/10.1371/journal.pone.0048230

Marlatt, G. A., & Donovan, D. M. (2017). *Relapse prevention: Maintenance strategies in the treatment of addictive behaviors* (2nd ed.). Guilford Press.

Meyer, D., & Brown, J. (2017). Somatic approaches to trauma recovery: Clinical applications. *Journal of Bodywork & Movement Therapies, 21*(4), 748–755. https://doi.org/10.1016/j.jbmt.2017.05.004

Norris, A. E. (2006). Muscular armoring: A critical review of Reich's concept. *Journal of Bodywork & Movement Therapies, 10*(4), 345–352. https://doi.org/10.1016/j.jbmt.2005.09.005

Ogden, P. (2017). Somatic therapy and 12-Step recovery: A case series. *Journal of Body Psychotherapy, 11*(2), 85–103.

Ogden, P., Minton, K., & Pain, C. (2006). *Trauma and the body: A sensorimotor approach to psychotherapy.* W. W. Norton.

Payne, P., Levine, P. A., & Crane-Godreau, M. A. (2015). Somatic experiencing: Using interoception and proprioception as core elements of trauma therapy. *Frontiers in Psychology, 6,* 93. https://doi.org/10.3389/fpsyg.2015.00093

Porges, S. W. (2011). *The polyvagal theory: Neurophysiological foundations of emotions, attachment, communication, and self-regulation. Norton Series on Interpersonal Neurobiology.* W. W. Norton.

Reich, W. (1933). *Character analysis.* Orgone Institute Press.

Rosenberg, R. (1981). A review of Bioenergetic Analysis in trauma treatment. *American Journal of Psychotherapy, 35*(3), 467–478. https://doi.org/10.1176/ajp.35.3.467

Scaer, R. C. (2001). *The body bears the burden: Trauma, dissociation, and disease.* Routledge.

Schore, A. N. (2012). *The science of the art of psychotherapy: Neurobiology and clinical practice.* W. W. Norton.

Sensky, T. (2000). *Mindful recovery: A guide to healing from addiction.* Mindful Press.

Shapiro, F. (2014). *Eye movement desensitization and reprocessing (EMDR) therapy: Basic principles, protocols, and procedures* (2nd ed.). Guilford Press.

Smolarz, D. (2019). Somatic approaches in substance use treatment: A systematic review. *Journal of Addiction Medicine, 13*(6), e322–e330. https://doi.org/10.1097/ADM.0000000000000534

Soth, M., & Stiles, P. (1998). *Somatic and transpersonal therapy: A psychological perspective.* Brown & Benchmark.

Steinberger, L., et al. (2020). Embodied spirituality: Integrating somatic practices in contemporary spiritual care. *Journal of Pastoral Theology, 30*(2), 85–102. https://doi.org/10.1080/08854726.2020.1741841

Teicher, M. H., Anderson, C. M., & Polcari, A. (2003). The neurobiological consequences of early stress and childhood maltreatment. *Neuroscience & Biobehavioral Reviews, 27*(1–2), 33–44. https://doi.org/10.1016/S0149-7634(03)00007-1

Van der Kolk, B. A. (2005). Developmental trauma disorder: A proposal for inclusion in DSM-V. *Psychiatric Annals, 35*(5), 401–408. https://doi.org/10.3928/00485713-

20050501-06

Van der Kolk, B. A. (2014). *The body keeps the score: Brain, mind, and body in the healing of trauma*. Penguin Books.

Vaughan, A., & Cooper, T. (2016). Reiki in substance use treatment: A systematic review. *Complementary Therapies in Medicine, 28,* 81–86. https://doi.org/10.1016/j.ctim.2016.05.003

Walker, E. A., Unutzer, J., Rutter, C., Gelfand, A., Saunders, K. E., VonKorff, M., Koss, M. P., & Katon, W. (1999). Costs of health care use by women HMO members with a history of childhood abuse and neglect. *Archives of General Psychiatry, 56*(7), 609–613. https://doi.org/10.1001/archpsyc.56.7.609

Winhall, J., & Porges, S. W. (2020). Revolutionizing addiction treatment with the felt sense polyvagal model. *International Body Psychotherapy Journal, 19*(1), 23–34. http://www.ibpj.org/issues/articles/Jan%20Winhall,%20Stephen%20W.%20Porges%20-%20Revolutionizing%20Addiction%20Treatment.pdf

Winnicott, D. W. (1960). The theory of the parent-infant relationship. *International Journal of Psychoanalysis, 41,* 585–595.

www.ingramcontent.com/pod-product-compliance
Lightning Source LLC
Chambersburg PA
CBHW051923160426
43198CB00012B/2014